LET GOD BE TRUE:
AND EVERY MAN A LIAR

Salvation God's Way
Pursuing Truth Over Tradition

All rights reserved.

Copyright © 2023

No part of this book may be reproduced or transmitted in any form or by any means, electronic or mechanical, including photocopying, recording or by an information storage and retrieval system – except by a reviewer who may quote brief passages in a magazine, newspaper, or on the web – without permission in writing from the publisher.

Scripture quotations marked (ESV) are from the ESV® Bible (The Holy Bible, English Standard Version®), copyright © 2001 by Crossway, a publishing ministry of Good News Publishers. Used by permission. All rights reserved.

Scripture quotations from The Authorized (King James) Version. Rights in the Authorized Version in the United Kingdom are vested in the Crown. Reproduced by permission of the Crown's patentee, Cambridge University Press

To my daughters,
Jubilee Ryan and ***Jenevieve Eden.***

God made you in His image, and His image is perfect.

Table of Contents

Preface 7

1 Common Ground vs. Battle Ground 11

2 The Door of Salvation 19

3 Jesus 33

4 History is His Story Part 1 45

5 History is His-Story Part 2 65

6 Kingdom of the Second-Born 79

7 To Work or Not to Work 95

8 Letters to the Bride 113

9 A New Name 125

10 The Gift 149

11 Born to Live 161

Preface

To write or not to write? This is the question I've struggled with for the past two years. I felt I needed to write, however; I felt incapable of doing so. I wrestled with insecurities and inabilities; I am not a great writer, nor even a good one.

In the world of Christian writers, I'm a small minnow in a great lake; a tiny pebble in a formation of mountains. This was the struggle. Feeling God led me to write and knowing I am grossly unqualified to do so.

So many great men and women I look up to and consider next level leaders are miles ahead of me in experience, knowledge, and ability, yet they've never written a book. If they haven't felt the need to write, then why should I think I have something to say? This question, among others, halted me frequently during the writing of this book.

I still don't know the answers to these questions; why would God lead me to write a book when there are hundreds of others who are more accomplished and definitely more able than myself?

I didn't write this book because I thought I had something good to say. Rather, I wrote because I felt God wanted me to.

I read an article about how to write a good preface, and one point they gave to add to a good preface was to include why you are qualified to write about the appointed topic. That's the problem. I'm unqualified in almost every way.

That, I confess, is the reason it took me so long to write this book. Two long years of writing for a few days, then allowing insecurity to stop me for months at a time. But here we are. I finished the book and I pray it can be a blessing for those sincere in their search for the truth of God's word.

There are so many traditions that have become deeply rooted in our Christian faith; traditions so many faithfully follow without ever taking the time and effort to confirm if they're actually biblical. I fear that many tread on the heels of these traditions with the sincere belief that God will honor their commitment to said traditions.

But traditions do not save. They never have and they never will. Only God has the power to save. If we live by that philosophy, then we can say the same about every religion across the world with devoted constituents. Surely God will honor those people for having a genuine faithfulness to what they deem as truth? That's not what God's word tells us. Rather, we read in scripture that there is only one door to eternal salvation, and it is through Jesus Christ.

We must not blindly follow man's tradition. We must discover God's truth. When we find the truth, the truth shall make us free.

We must do more than just learn truth; we must love truth. If you love something, you commit yourself to it; you build your life on it; you let it determine your future.

I am forever thankful for my parents; they showed me how to fall in love with God and His word; they showed me what it looks like betting it all on God; to take Him at His word; to trust in His plans and surrender to His will.

This topic I felt compelled to write about, New Testament salvation, is a topic that means so much to me. I don't go a day of my life without thinking about these biblical principles. They're always on my mind and forever in my heart. They are the foundation on which I'm building my marriage and family.

When the world becomes ever more unstable, God's word becomes ever more unmovable. With every new question the world presents, God's word has an answer for it. It's never outdated, it's always cutting edge. It doesn't grow weaker with time. Rather, it grows stronger. The Bible is one of the greatest gifts God gave to man; it has God for an author; salvation for its end; and enduring truth throughout.

President John Adams said, "I have examined all… and the result is that the Bible is the best book in the World." Throughout the last two millennia, men and women have looked to the Bible as the ultimate source of truth. Kingdoms have risen powerfully and fallen pitifully, but the Word of God has never fallen, rather it has continued to rise. Kings and peasants alike have lifted it; it has provided the bedrock on which people built the Republic of the United States of America. There's no other document in the history of mankind that has been as influential as the Bible. It has always been truth; it always will be truth.

I want to present a challenge to everybody everywhere: we should go back to the Bible and let that be the foundation for every area of our lives. Let it form our worldview and change our culture; let it bless our families; and let it save our souls.

I shout out my wife for being understanding, for allowing me to come home after a long day's work and spend hours writing. For supporting me during this process with which I struggled. I love my family dearly.

Who knows, nobody else may read these pages, and that's okay, because if only my daughters read this book and it somehow strengthens their confidence in God's word, then every moment of the process was worth it.

One of my greatest desires in life is to see my children grow up in the Lord, and to see them fall in love with the scriptures that have saved my life so many times. So join me, if you will, on this journey through the scriptures in search of the truth of God's word. Salvation is for everybody. There is no person too far, too low, or too lost. God can reach you. You can make it. He can save you, but it must be God's way.

1
Common Ground vs. Battle Ground

At any cost, heaven is going to be mighty affordable.

—Sam Emory

I have found that it's much more beneficial to begin with what we agree on before speaking about what we may disagree on. Finding a common ground can be the launching pad into revelation, while a battle ground leads to a bloody mess with one standing as victor and the other lying in defeat.

Too often we possess a battle ground attitude when discussing God's word. We step into the ring, ready to beat our opponent with our superior intellect. You may win an argument that way, but you'll never win a soul that way. Winning an argument should never be our intention when discussing the Word of God. If we enter a discussion with only the intention to "win" then we have already lost.

So, let's find common ground, something that all of Christendom should agree on; the infallible Word of God. Before moving on with our discussion, let's agree on this one thing: heaven and earth may pass away, but God's word will stand forever (Matt. 24:25). We must agree that God's word is true and, despite what any man says, His word is the ultimate authority. Paul wrote, "Let God be true and every man a liar" (Romans 3:4). We must believe that *all* scripture is given by inspiration of God and is profitable for doctrine (2 Tim. 3:16). If we do not believe these things, then we cannot move any further, because to doubt the legitimacy of one portion of scripture brings the entire collection of holy scriptures into question.

We must believe that God's word is true, and the ultimate authority for our doctrine and, most importantly, our salvation. Meaning, I cannot put my eternity in the hands of what man preaches; I must follow what His word teaches.

I am not interested in winning an argument. I sincerely want to know the truth of God's word. When Jesus returns for a church that has made herself ready, I want to be a part of that glorious meeting in the air. I'm not interested in playing God-games. If you're okay with jumping and skipping through life with a happy-go-lucky attitude without ever stopping to think about what God desires from us, or how He wants us to live our life, then we're not on common ground.

I believe that two of the most important questions in life are: "Is there a God?" and if the answer to that question is yes, then the next important question is, "What does He require of me?" You cannot believe God exists but live as though He doesn't. If God truly exists, then we have a major obligation to find out what His purpose is in giving us life.

If you believe God is real, you must then ask, "what is my responsibility to Him?" If God is the only reason you're living; if it's by His graceful permission that your heart still beats, then we must acknowledge that He has a purpose for us. What is His will for us? What does He desire from us?

Craig Groeschel wrote a book entitled *The Christian Atheist: Believing in God but Living As If He Doesn't Exist*. While I haven't read the book, the title and subtitle stick out to me. If God is real, then He has created us on purpose for a purpose. We must acknowledge His existence, and diligently search for His will.

It's dangerous to believe in God, but live ignorant of His purpose; to acknowledge God in your mind and ignore Him in your life.

If I believe Jesus was the Son of God and that He died for our sins, I'm compelled to ask the important questions. I must do more than simply acknowledge God's existence. I must seek His purpose.

The truth is this: He gave His life for us, so we may give our life to Him. You are alive for a reason; it is God's reason. In a way, this book is exploring these questions. What is God's will for me? What does God desire of me? And what is His plan for us?

I believe Jesus is real, and that He is the savior of the world. I'm convinced that Jesus has prepared a place for me, a place of eternity in His presence. More than anything, I want to make sure I'm ready, and that my family is ready.

Heaven is much too important to me to treat living for God as a game. So, if we continue together on this journey to uncover the truth of His word, then I assume that, like me, you are sincere in your search for the true salvation Jesus has made available to us.

I am honored and humbled that you chose to give this book your time; I pray you are blessed and ministered to.

Something Doesn't Add Up

We have a major crisis. Paul wrote in Ephesians 4:5, "One Lord, one faith, one baptism." Paul puts an emphasis on the singularity of the Gospel. He makes it very plain that there is only one faith, however research reveals that there are over 200 major denominations within Protestant Christianity, most of which have their own beliefs on salvation. Some denominations teach baptism is necessary, while others say it isn't; some say works have nothing to do with salvation, others say that works do matter. Some say just believe and others say belief isn't enough; some baptize infants and some see that as invalid. Some baptize with full immersion while others just sprinkle; some speak in tongues, while others think speaking in tongues is irrelevant and foolish. Many say once you experience salvation that you are set for life and never have to worry about losing out, others say that just like you obtain salvation, you can lose your salvation, and many more beliefs.

Something doesn't add up. Was Paul wrong in his writing? Is there more than one faith? Either God's word is false, or there are many people who are very confused. God's word is never wrong; therefore, we must work hard to maneuver through this massive array of ever-changing beliefs regarding salvation and build our house firmly on the rock of God's word, and declare that His word is the ultimate truth. This is what the apostle Paul writes:

> *So that we may no longer be children, tossed to and fro by the waves and carried about by every wind of doctrine, by human cunning, by craftiness in deceitful schemes. Rather, speaking the truth in love, we are to grow up in every way into him who is the head, into Christ.*
>
> **Ephesians 4:14–15 (ESV)**

He warns us of the danger found in the "winds of doctrine." He says that the doctrines made by man shouldn't manipulate or carry us off, rather, we should speak the truth in love and grow up into Christ.

We should firmly plant our lives in the Word of God, and not in the traditions of man. We should grow in Christ and not in tradition. We should put our trust in what Jesus said, and not what modern Christianity says. There are many "winds of doctrine" pushing people off course. Many pastors and preachers are more concerned with how much money you can give them than with your eternal salvation.

That's why Paul says this:

> *God forbid: yea, let God be true, but every man a liar…*
>
> **Romans 3:4 (KJV)**

God is truth. His word is truth. We cannot allow ourselves to trust man more than God. Put your trust in the Bible, grab the scriptures with both hands, and hold on tight. It will not fail you.

The World's Picture vs God's Picture

In Matthew 7, Jesus draws us a picture of two gates, one narrow and one wide.

Enter ye in at the strait gate: for wide is the gate, and broad is the way, that leadeth to destruction, and many there be which go in thereat: Because strait is the gate, and narrow is the way, which leadeth unto life, and few there be that find it.

Matthew 7:13–14 (KJV)

The Christian world can paint a picture of a road to heaven that is so wide it's impossible to miss. However, Jesus presents just the opposite, with the road of destruction being the wider gate with many entering; and the narrow gate, the one only the few find, being the road leading to eternal life. That tells me I must be intentional about finding the correct gate and choosing to enter there.

Salvation must not be an afterthought, but it should consume our mind and our thinking. Jesus says not everyone that says Lord, Lord, will enter heaven, but it's those that do the will of Him who are in heaven. Jesus talks about those who will stand before His throne as He gives the verdict:

Many will say to me in that day, Lord, Lord, have we not prophesied in thy name? and in thy name have cast out devils? and in thy name done many wonderful works? And then will I profess unto them, I never knew you: depart from me, ye that work iniquity.

Matthew 7:22–23 (KJV)

These will be men and women that have prophesied, cast out devils, and done many wonderful works, not in the name of a false god, but in His name. These people knew the name of Jesus, used and exercised the name of Jesus, yet, nevertheless, the Lord professes to them, "I never knew you, depart from me ye that work iniquity."

I don't know how this makes you feel, but this vivid scene in the scripture scares me. To think that after teaching, preaching, and doing everything I do, I can end in failure because there was something lacking.

After all, they had prophesied and cast out devils! They apparently weren't powerless; they possessed enough anointing to cast out the devils. Others in the Bible had tried to do the same using the name of Jesus, and they failed. So, they certainly had the power of the name of Jesus. They had also done many wonderful works. Sounds to me as though they were the "cream of the crop."

So, what went wrong? Through the lens of modern Christianity, that group would've been the first in line. They would've been the above and beyond group, but Jesus didn't see it that way. Jesus lets us know that there's more to salvation than just knowing and believing in His name.

God's picture of salvation seems pretty narrow, so why does the world paint this portrait of a salvation so wide and so inclusive that one could sleepwalk their way into the gates of heaven? We must not follow our traditions, we must find out what God's word says about our salvation and follow it. Purchase your ticket from the Word of God and not from a preacher behind the pulpit.

In the following chapters, we're going to uncover not my opinions but God's truths regarding salvation. He didn't make it cloudy and unclear, quite the contrary. His salvation plan is laid out beautifully yet plainly; you will find that once you take God at His word, there is no confusion.

2

The Door of Salvation

Jesus is not one of many ways to approach God, nor is He the best of several ways; He is the only way.

—**A. W. Tozer**

Doors are places of transition. They transport us from one room to another. A doorway is the entrance to a new space, and one cannot enter a new space without first exiting the previous. Jesus is the door that leads to truth and to life. We must leave the room of tradition and enter the doorway of truth.

In this chapter, I want to present what I believe the Bible clearly teaches regarding salvation. If I may, I will use this chapter to lay a scriptural foundation regarding Bible salvation. All the chapters following this one will be a scriptural defense or case to support these claims biblically.

If you do not agree with the claims I make in this chapter, or if you have any objections, then I ask that you stick with me and hopefully I will address your objections or concerns in the following chapters.

Salvation should never be an afterthought, rather, it should be our top priority. Spending eternity in heaven with the Lord, Jesus Christ, is the supreme goal of life. Our trust should not be in tradition or in man, but in Christ and in His words. King David said, "Thy word is a lamp to my feet and a light to my path."

Let God's word be the light for your path; let God's word establish the direction of your life. I pray that together we can draw closer to the truth of God's word, for His word is life everlasting. In His word, there is peace for your mind and joy for your spirit.

Jesus is the Door

Let's begin once again with common ground. I believe Jesus Christ is the *only* way. Outside of Jesus, there is no salvation. We find life in Him, and Him alone. Any direction that leads away from Christ is the wrong direction. Jesus is the only way out of sin. Jesus is the only answer to this lost world. There are not many ways; there is only one way. Jesus.

He is the captain of our salvation; He is the one who makes us new. Only by the grace of our great God are we saved. Without the Lord, we are lost and broken. If we were left to our own, we'd all end up in destruction; but thanks be to God, He didn't leave us alone! He came to save and redeem us. It was Jesus that made salvation possible, and nobody else can do for this world what Jesus did for this world. Jesus is the only salvation.

Jesus didn't leave us a mystery regarding salvation. He spoke clearly and plainly, telling people He was the only option for salvation.

Jesus saith unto him, I am the way, the truth, and the life: no man cometh unto the Father, but by me.

John 14:6 (KJV)

Whenever Jesus claims to be "the way," He is exclusive in His claims. He doesn't present Himself as one of many ways, but as the only way. Even saying that no man can come to God unless they come through Him. Not only did Jesus say He was the only way, Jesus likened His way to a door.

I am the door: by me if any man enter in, he shall be saved, and shall go in and out, and find pasture.

John 10:9 (KJV)

Jesus was also exclusive in this statement. He did not say "I am a door." Nor did He say, "I am one of the doors." Jesus said, "I am *THE* door." If you enter into Him; if you walk through His door, you will be saved, and if that is true, then the opposite is true: if you do not enter His door, then you will not be saved. Outside of Jesus, we are lost, but in Jesus, we are saved.

Jesus is the door. There is not another door in this life that can save you. There is not another gospel that can take what's broken and make it whole again. Like Paul, I am unashamed of the Gospel of Christ. Why? It has saved a wretch like me. It took my meaningless life and gave it meaning and purpose.

His story of mercy and grace redeemed my story that was full of shame and regret. I once was addicted, locked in a room of depression, but Jesus brought me out. In my room of darkness, He was the door that brought me into the light.

There is no situation that He cannot make a way out of. He can be the door out of your emotional trauma. He can be the door out of your anxiety and fear. He can be the door out of depression and suicidal thoughts. How do I know? He did it for me and He did it for my wife.

Time fails me to tell the testimonies of people in my life, that were so extremely broken until Jesus entered the picture. There is a door out of drug and alcohol addiction. It's Jesus. When I was lost in sin, Jesus opened His arms and welcomingly invited me into a new life. The same can be true for you, and for anybody else in this world. The message of Bible salvation is clear—look to Jesus.

It's so important that we know who the door is. The door is Jesus Christ. Hopefully, we can find common ground there, because if you don't believe that Jesus is the only salvation, the course of our conversation would need to take a new direction. Before you can discover His plan, you must discover Him.

Some may say something like this: "all ladders reach the top." However, that's not what the Bible teaches. The only ladder that reaches heaven is Jesus's ladder. Jesus did not practice or promote religious tolerance. He was very adamant that there is only one God and that every other is false. There is, absolutely, a door of salvation; and that door is Jesus.

Through the Door

If we agree on who the door is, we can move on to the next point of discussion. How does one walk through the door of salvation? How does one enter Christ and His body? Do we walk through the door into Christ's salvation by belief alone? Is it faith alone that brings us over the threshold of salvation's door? Out of sin and into righteousness? Modern day Christianity would say yes, but I believe the Bible clearly teaches otherwise.

Again, in this chapter, I will only present what I believe to be Bible salvation, paired with minimal scriptures and a brief explanation. I will dedicate the rest of this book to proving and providing a more detailed explanation of the claims I make in this chapter.

Your belief in Jesus is *not* enough to walk through His door. Jesus said this:

Then said Jesus unto his disciples, If any man will come after me, let him deny himself, and take up his cross, and follow me.

Matthew 16:24 (KJV)

There is action that we must pair with our faith. There is a biblical response to the Gospel, a response the Lord has established as necessary to enter the new covenant bride of Christ. That response is taking up your cross. After all, it was His cross that tore the veil and opened the door of salvation, and it is our cross that brings us through the door.

Our cross isn't different from His cross. While we don't struggle under the physical weight of a literal tree, our cross will take us through the same journey Jesus took during His crucifixion. Our cross is a direct reflection of His cross. Our experience will be a direct parallel to His experience. The only difference being His experience was physical, and ours is spiritual.

- Jesus died on the cross physically—and we must die on the cross spiritually.
- Jesus was buried physically—we must be buried spiritually.
- Jesus was resurrected physically—we must be resurrected spiritually.

That's why Paul says things like this:

<u>I am crucified with Christ</u>: nevertheless I live...
Galatians 2:20 (KJV)

<u>Buried with him</u> in baptism, wherein <u>also ye are risen with him</u> through the faith of the operation of God, who hath raised him from the dead.
Colossians 2:12 (KJV)

If the Spirit of him who raised Jesus from the dead dwells in you, he who raised Christ Jesus from the dead <u>will also give life to your mortal bodies through his Spirit who dwells in you.</u>
Romans 8:11 (ESV)

It is a faithful saying: For if we be dead with him, we shall also live with him:
2 Timothy 2:11 (KJV)

There are more scripture passages we could visit together, and we will go through them in the following chapters. However, with these few verses, Paul directly identifies his conversion with Christ's crucifixion. Paul says, "I am crucified with Christ," "Buried with Him," "Risen with Him," and so on.

This is a beautiful picture of Paul describing what it means to take up your own cross to follow Jesus. Jesus didn't give us a multiple-choice question, rather a singular and direct challenge. "If you want to follow me… take up your cross."

His cross opened the door of salvation. Our cross brings us through the door of salvation. Believing in the door won't bring you through the door. The only way to go through the door is to go through in the same manner Jesus went through. Death, burial, and resurrection.

The question I will circle in this book is this: "how can we be saved?" Here is the most clear-cut answer I can give you. You must repent of your sins, and be water baptized in the name of Jesus Christ for the remission of your sins, and receive the gift of the Holy Ghost.

IMPORTANT DISCLAIMER! This is not my opinion. I pulled this directly from the divine library of God's written words. This is a response from the Apostle Peter when a man asked him the same question in response to hearing the Gospel, "What Must I Do?" Here is the verse:

Now when they heard this, they were pricked in their heart, and said unto Peter and to the rest of the apostles, Men and brethren, what shall we do? Then Peter said unto them, Repent, and be baptized every one of you in the name of Jesus Christ for the remission of sins, and ye shall receive the gift of the Holy Ghost.

Acts 2:37–38 (KJV)

Peter's answer is a direct parallel with the crucifixion of Jesus Christ. Peter is saying the same thing Jesus said. If you want to follow Jesus, you must take up your cross. The steps that Peter gave in that verse exactly correlate with the experience of Jesus's crucifixion.

- Repent of your sins — Death. (Romans 6:7, 11)
- Water Baptism in Jesus Name — Burial. (Romans 6:3–4)
- Being filled with the Spirit — Resurrection. (Romans 6:5–8)

You see, it was His cross that opened the door, and it is our cross that brings us through the door. This is why Jesus said, "If any man will come after me, let him deny himself, and take up his cross, and follow me." You cannot be saved if you don't carry your own cross and align yourself with the perfect example given to us by our perfect savior. You must believe in Christ and obey Christ. Do not reject the cross, rather, embrace it. Repent of your sins and be baptized in the name of Jesus, and receive the gift of the Holy Ghost. You can be saved, but it *must* be through Jesus.

We must do something about the cross, and one of two things only can we do — flee it or die upon it.

—A. W. Tozer

Blood, Water and Spirit

Let's zoom in on this picture of the cross, and magnify those three experiences of the cross and of New Testament salvation. The death, the burial, and the resurrection. There is another way the Bible speaks of these: we have three components of salvation that are inseparable from the three experiences of salvation. We identify them as blood, water, and the Spirit. These three components correspond with the experiences of the cross. They are inseparable from our salvation. They are the very tools God chose to use for the purpose of salvation. Here is what John said in his first letter:

> *This is he who came by <u>water and blood</u>—Jesus Christ; <u>not by the water only but by the water and the blood</u>. <u>And the Spirit</u> is the one who testifies, because the Spirit is the truth. <u>For there are three that testify</u>: <u>the Spirit and the water and the blood; and these three agree</u>. If we receive the testimony of men, the testimony of God is greater, for this is the testimony of God that he has borne concerning his Son.*
>
> **1 John 5:6–9 (ESV)**

The testimony of God, according to John, is the Spirit and the water and the blood. John said these three components agree together as one. They are the testimony or witness of heaven.

We certainly should find common ground on the importance of the blood of Jesus. It is by His blood that we are saved. The tragic fact is this: we are all tainted by sin. We all have made mistakes and fallen short of goodness and righteousness, and because of that, we all owe the penalty of sin.

Let me use this analogy. We sat at the table and ordered the food. We are the ones who ate what was on plate. Therefore, it is we who are responsible for paying the bill. Not anybody else, just ourselves. Sin demanded our blood, and our life as payment for our sins, but God, who is rich in mercy, stepped in and paid the bill we owed. When sin demanded our blood, Jesus offered His blood instead.

The only reason we can be free from the penalty of sin is because of the blood of Jesus Christ! The blood that was, in fact, shed on THE CROSS! You see, we find our salvation in Jesus, His cross and His blood! Here are a few verses of scripture:

But if we walk in the light, as he is in the light, we have fellowship with one another, and <u>the blood of Jesus his Son cleanses us from all sin.</u>

1 John 1:7 (ESV)

And they have conquered him <u>by the blood of the Lamb</u> and by the word of their testimony, for they loved not their lives even unto death.

Revelation 12:11 (ESV)

<u>In him</u> we have redemption <u>through his blood</u>, the forgiveness of our trespasses, according to the riches of his grace.

Ephesians 1:7 (ESV)

The common ground is here. We can agree that the blood of Jesus, shed on the cross of calvary, is what gives us redemption and forgiveness of sins.

Let's take it further, because the testimony of God is not blood only, but also water and Spirit. Jesus said this:

> *Jesus answered, Verily, verily, I say unto thee, Except a man be born of water and of the Spirit, he cannot enter into the kingdom of God.*
>
> **John 3:5 (KJV)**

Without being born of water and of Spirit, we cannot enter the kingdom of God. The blood that was shed on the cross is not the entire story, but Jesus said we must be born of water and of the Spirit. These three components of New Testament salvation work together to form what John called, "the testimony of God." There will be more on this in chapter 9 "A New Name," but let me just say that to be born of water means being water baptized in Jesus's name, and to be born of the Spirit means being filled with God's spirit. The three components of New Testament salvation are blood, water, and the Spirit; and they all flow out of Jesus on the cross.

So, Jesus is the door of salvation. It was His experience on the cross that opened the door of salvation, and it is our experience with the cross that brings us into salvation. When Jesus died on the cross, all three components of New Testament salvation flowed out of Him.

> *When Jesus had received the sour wine, he said, "It is finished," and he bowed his head and <u>gave up his spirit</u>.*
>
> **John 19:30 (ESV)**

But one of the soldiers pierced his side with a spear, and at once there came out blood and water.

John 19:34 (ESV)

The picture of the cross is not a pretty one. Jesus had been beaten, tortured, crucified. He willingly submitted to this treatment because He loved the world, and wanted to save the people He cared so much for from the sin that was destroying them. And so, He goes to the cross to crush sin. To open the door of salvation that had been closed for centuries.

In His last moment of life, the Bible says Jesus gave up His Spirit, meaning he died. The Spirit of the body left the body. When the soldier saw Jesus was dead, he stabbed Jesus in the side with his spear and when he plunged the spear into the side of Jesus, blood and water immediately flowed out.

When Jesus died on the cross, blood, water and Spirit all flowed out of Him. We know the cross opened the door, and we enter by the cross. Out of the cross flows blood, water, and Spirit. We cannot take up the cross without being willing to receive the blood, water, and Spirit that flows from the cross. We cannot enter the door of salvation without blood, water, and Spirit.

New Testament Salvation (Acts 2:38)

- Death—Blood—Repentance.
- Burial—Water—Baptism.
- Resurrection—Spirit—Filled the Holy Spirit.

You can be saved. It doesn't matter who you are or how far you've fallen. The blood of Jesus Christ can reach you. His grace is sufficient for you. His mercy is new every morning. Salvation is available to you.

You don't have to be rich; you don't have to have prestige; you don't have to have it all together. You only need to be willing to look to Jesus, look to His cross, and follow His example. It was through His cross that salvation came to us, and it is through our cross that we come to salvation. I hope you will continue to take this journey with me through the unparalleled words of God's Holy book, and always remember—let God be true, and every man a liar.

"Know ye not, that so many of us as were baptized into Jesus Christ were baptized into his death? Therefore we are buried with him by baptism into death: that like as Christ was raised up from the dead by the glory of the Father, even so we also should walk in newness of life. For if we have been planted together in the likeness of his death, we shall be also in the likeness of his resurrection: Knowing this, that our old man is crucified with him, that the body of sin might be destroyed, that henceforth we should not serve sin. For he that is dead is freed from sin. 8. Now if we be dead with Christ, we believe that we shall also live with him…"

Romans 6:3–8 (KJV)

3
Jesus

Follow me, as I follow Christ.

—The Apostle Paul

To be like Jesus, to be like Jesus, on earth I long to be like Him. All through life's journey, from earth to glory, I only ask to be like Him.

Isn't that our greatest desire? To be like Jesus, to be made in His glorious image, to follow His perfect example, to share His unparalleled message of hope. To live as He lived, to love as He loved, and yes, to teach what He taught. Which is what? Before we look anywhere else for answers regarding salvation, we should first look at Jesus. What did Jesus teach? How did He live? What examples did He leave from His life for us to follow?

To be completely honest, I am surprised by the tremendous amount of confusion regarding this subject. When I read the

Gospels, the red letters seem extraordinarily clear. Jesus didn't leave us with a complicated riddle to unravel, but he spoke precisely regarding what's necessary to make it to heaven.

He also showed us how through His life on earth. So, I pray you keep an open mind as we take a closer look at the life and ministry of our Lord Jesus Christ.

John the Baptist

Jesus's ministry was preceded by the ministry of His cousin, John the Baptist. He was "the voice crying in the wilderness, prepare ye the way of the Lord."

John the Baptist came preaching baptism unto repentance. He spent his days in the wilderness preaching and baptizing. Multitudes came to hear this new teaching of repentance and to be baptized in the river.

It was new because never before was it an option to just pray and confess your sins and have God forgive them. Prayer was definitely available, but forgiveness of sins always followed an altar with a burnt offering. It always happened after a blood sacrifice. So, this idea was new. The idea that John was preaching was giving us a picture of what was to come.

Jesus did *not* reject this new teaching. And this, I believe, is so important. Because Jesus is everything, He is our example; He is our savior; He is our redeemer; He is the one who made a way for sinners to be saved, and we cannot call ourselves Christians if we don't follow His example. We cannot accept a teacher and not accept His teachings. If Jesus was against it, then we, too, should be against it. And if Jesus was for it, then we, too, should be for it.

There is one thing that Jesus was very much for, and that is baptism. He not only approved of it, but He took part in it. He came to John and told John to baptize Him. We must not overlook the fact that Jesus Himself was baptized. We are going to look at it more closely in a moment, but first, let me say this: if Jesus Christ, who is God wrapped up in a body, who had all power in heaven and in earth, who was without sin, who was perfect in wisdom, and completely righteous. If He needed to be baptized, then so do we.

It doesn't matter who says they don't need it. Jesus is my perfect example. If He needed it, then I need it. I am not baptized because a preacher told me to be. I am baptized because Jesus set the example and anything less than that; I am not interested in.

The mission of John the Baptist was to prepare "the way of the Lord," and he clearly focused his message on repentance and baptism. "The way" that John prepared was a message of repentance and baptism. John preached to the people, "You need to repent and you need to be baptized." When Jesus finally arrives, He embraces John's message and John baptizes Him.

Notice how awkward it would have been if John had spent his life preparing the way for Jesus, only for Jesus to walk a different way. If John spent his years in the wilderness, passionately preaching that one must be baptized, only for Jesus to arrive and say it wasn't necessary.

It would be an unfortunate scene in time to have the "wrong way" prepared for the Messiah. However, when Jesus arrived at the scene, He did not sidestep the message of John, but He embraced it and walked in it.

In this next section, we will read about the first encounter Jesus has with John the Baptist. But understand this one important principle. John prepared the way, Jesus showed the way, and we follow the way.

Jesus with John the Baptist

The conversation that takes place that day between John and Jesus is powerful on many points. It gives a clear picture of what Jesus felt was important.

The scene began that morning. John was busy preaching to the many men and women who came to hear him. His rough style and new ideas attracted many who were sincerely ready to get out of their rituals and religion. They wanted a God they could understand. The feasts, the ceremonies, the sacrifices, everything they had learned from their childhood about a God who was out of touch. A God who was unapproachable to the normal populace. A Mighty God, who rules from His throne in heaven. They couldn't come close to Him or interact with Him because they weren't priests and hadn't been consecrated with blood and anointing oil. They didn't wear the ephod, and they didn't work in the temple, so they were taught to trust the priest.

Just live your lives and bring your offerings, and let the priests do business with God. But there was John. John didn't work in the temple, but God still spoke to him. He didn't wear the priestly garments, but somehow he interacted with God, and that brought people from far and wide. Because they wanted to be a part of what God was doing. They wanted to experience God for themselves! It's not enough to just sit back and leave the "God stuff" to the priests. My family needs God.

John was preaching, and the people were receiving his words and accepting baptism, when a newcomer joined the crowd and immediately the Spirit of God gives John revelation. John cries out, "Behold the Lamb of God which takes away the sins of the world"—everybody LOOK! This is what you have come for! This is the Lamb of God! This is God with us! This man is the answer to every one of our questions! He is the answer to all our prayers! He is the one who will take away your sins! Take your eyes off of me and look at Him! He is your SALVATION! Behold the Lamb of God!

The crowd placed their full attention on Jesus. All eyes were on Him. The whispers and the excitement that rose in the crowd. Could it be that He was the one? The crowd parted, making way for Jesus as He walked directly to John, His lips shaped to form a word and the crowd hushed, straining to hear what Jesus would say!

His entrance was epic, His introduction was immense, and everybody wanted to hear what the Lamb of God would say! And to the surprise of the crowd and to John, Jesus said, "I need to be baptized by you."

Out of everything Jesus could've said in that moment, He was the living Word incarnate, and He could've spoke a new word. He could've preached a sermon. He could've healed some sick folk. But instead, He told John, "Baptize me."

John, of course, starts by refusing. Because, after all, who was he to baptize the Lamb of God? John tells Jesus, "No, I need to be baptized by you."

It's true that any of us would've said the same thing. If the Messiah walked up to us while standing in a river and asked us to baptize Him, I believe we'd respond similarly. No, no, no, Jesus, there's no way I'm good enough to baptize you. You need to baptize me! That is where John was, in that moment, but Jesus responded with something we should think about.

> *John would have prevented him, saying, 'I need to be baptized by you, and do you come to me?' But Jesus answered him, "Let it be so now, for thus it is fitting for us to fulfill all righteousness." Then he consented.*
>
> **Matthew 3:14–15 (ESV)**

Jesus said you need to baptize me so we can fulfill all righteousness. Jesus was adamant about being baptized, because without baptism, His example of how to fulfill righteousness as a human would've been incomplete. Telling me I cannot fulfill the righteousness in me unless I am baptized in water. That's not something we've made up and fabricated, but the words spoken by Jesus. "Lord, how can I possibly baptize you? Because, John, we need it to fulfill all righteousness."

With this, I will begin submitting that water baptism is an important and necessary component of God's salvation plan on earth. Without it, the process is incomplete. We cannot fulfill righteousness without baptism.

Jesus's Words

Jesus spoke of baptism in multiple places in the Gospel stories. Probably the most well-known across the Christian movement is John chapter 3.

In this chapter, a man of the pharisees, Nicodemus, came to Jesus by night with questions regarding the kingdom of God, and Jesus responds with a sentence that confuses Nicodemus.

Jesus answered him, "Truly, truly, I say to you, unless one is born again he cannot see the kingdom of God."
John 3:3 (ESV)

That thoroughly confused Nicodemus. What does this mean? To be born again? I cannot make it into the Kingdom of God without being born again? How does one be born again?

Nicodemus said to him, "How can a man be born when he is old? Can he enter a second time into his mother's womb and be born?"
John 3:4 (ESV)

His confusion is clear. He's thinking that to be born again somehow means to be reborn physically. But Jesus isn't talking about a natural birth, He is speaking of a spiritual birth. Our natural birth does not save us, but our spiritual birth does. If we are going to be saved, it won't come from natural causes, but it will happen through the Spirit.

Jesus then responds and clears up the confusion. He elaborates more on what being "born again" really means.

Jesus answered, "Truly, truly, I say to you, unless one is born of water and the Spirit, he cannot enter the kingdom of God."
John 3:5 (ESV)

To be "born again" is broken up in two parts, being born of water and the Spirit. And this process is so important Jesus said that unless it happens, one cannot enter the kingdom of God. There's no room for other options. Jesus said they cannot be a part of His kingdom unless they are born again. But what does being born of the water mean? And what about being born of the Spirit?

Let's start with being born of the water. Some believe that it refers to a natural birth. I had a conversation with a Baptist pastor one evening, and in discussing this passage he told me it referred to a natural birth, but I disagree with that conclusion, because I can find nowhere else in the Bible where a natural birth is referred to as being "born of water." Born of a woman? Yes. But never born of water.

So, there's no scriptural backing for this concept, and it takes a lot of stretching to make that fit into the scriptures. It also isn't interpreted that way by many early church fathers. Then what does it mean?

When compared to the rest of the teachings of Jesus and the Apostles, it's very clear that Jesus was referring to baptism by water and baptism by the Spirit. We can go to other locations where Jesus spoke about the kingdom and salvation and we can use the scriptures to show us what it means.

One of the clearest verses is in the Gospel of Mark. Jesus says this:

Whoever believes and is baptized will be saved, but whoever does not believe will be condemned.

Mark 16:16 (ESV)

This verse is astounding today because the modern Christian movement says believing in Jesus saves you. They say that salvation is by grace alone. Just believe in Jesus and He will save you. Jesus doesn't agree. Jesus said that whoever believes and is baptized will be saved. This is how important baptism was and is to Jesus.

Not only was Jesus baptized, and not only did He preach and teach baptism, but Jesus baptized (through His disciples.)

Now when Jesus learned that the Pharisees had heard that Jesus was making and baptizing more disciples than John, (although Jesus himself did not baptize, but only his disciples).

John 4:1–2 (ESV)

Jesus and the disciples were baptizing more than John had baptized. It was a major part of His ministry, and it was no doubt integral in His message.

Let me clarify this one thing: we don't believe our works save us. Jesus, and Him alone, saves us. The truth is, I can never be good enough to deserve salvation, and considering that truth, we understand that His grace is the only reason we can be saved. However, Jesus was clear on this one, equally true fact. He requires our obedience. Jesus said this in John 14:

If ye love me, keep my commandments.

John 14:15 (KJV)

While salvation is built on Jesus and His grace, it requires our faith and obedience to live in that salvation. Biblical faith requires obedience, faith without obedience is not biblical faith. We look at this more in the later chapter 7 "To Work or not to Work." Allow me to continue a little further with the words of Christ. Consider what Jesus says in John chapter 8:

Then said Jesus to those Jews which believed on him, If ye continue in my word, then are ye my disciples indeed; And ye shall know the truth, and the truth shall make you free.

John 8:31–32 (KJV)

Jesus throws out a pretty big "if." He tells the new believers, if you continue in my words, then are you my disciples indeed. Believing in Christ was not enough to be a disciple of Christ. Jesus plainly pronounces, you must also continue in my word. If you do not follow Jesus's teachings, you cannot be Jesus's disciple.

He finishes with one of my favorite verses in the Bible; you shall know the truth and the truth shall make you free.

I didn't write this book for the sake of argument; I wrote it for the sake of truth. I truly, and with all sincerity, want to know the truth. I want to be saved and I want my beautiful children, whom I love with all my heart, to be saved. For their sake, I cannot blindly follow tradition. I must let God be true and every man be a liar.

Final Farewell

Last words. Last words are special. The family of those who have passed on treasure them. If a man or woman knows they only have a few moments left, they normally choose their words carefully and wisely. Knowing that what they said would be remembered and forever attached to their memory. Those with little time don't waste time. And they don't waste words. Which begs the question, what were Jesus's last words?

On the Mount called Olivet, Jesus stopped. The small crowd of believers that had been walking closely behind Him halted as well. There, at the ridge of the mount, Jesus turns to face this crowd. Included in the people were the eleven disciples, and Mary, the mother of Jesus. Jesus isn't as they had known Him before. He was resurrected. Just days prior, He was dead. Buried in a tomb. Wrapped in grave clothes. However, He stood before them very much alive.

The only sign that Jesus had been crucified were the holes in His hands and feet; the hole in His side; and the scars that layered HIs body. Small but strong reminders of the ultimate sacrifice that He had willingly given. Jesus only had a moment left with the disciples before He ascended into the clouded sky.

With His face to the crowd, Jesus opened His mouth to form His last words. The crowd strained to hear what their savior was saying; they were open and ready to receive His instructions. With a commanding yet comforting voice, The Lord spoke these words,

Go therefore and make disciples of all nations, baptizing them in the name of the Father and of the Son and of the Holy Spirit, teaching them to observe all that I have commanded you. And behold, I am with you always, to the end of the age.

Matthew 28:19–20 (ESV)

That was His last command, commonly known as the great commission. Jesus said, "go and make disciples…" Just as Jesus made disciples, they were to follow His example. He doesn't end there, but in the same breath, Jesus gives them the instructions. He voices the plan for how they were to make disciples, "… baptizing them," the last words of Jesus Christ, were a command for His followers to baptize.

Baptism was important enough to Jesus for Him to add it to His final farewell. I hope and pray that this book encourages you to take the things Jesus thought were important and make them important for you. Jesus is more than just our savior; He is our example. He is our pattern. He is our model. Follow Jesus and become like Jesus.

4
History is His Story
Part 1

If you want to understand today, you have to search yesterday.

—Pearl S. Buck

One can learn much from examining the past. Looking at history can give us clarity on present issues. American historian David McCullough said, "History is who we are and why we are the way we are." History can be a powerful tool to help build our present.

It's not my desire to speak of American History, or recent world events. Rather, biblical history is what I believe holds boundless treasures for us in our spiritual life and walk with God. More specifically, what we call the Old Testament.

Some in the Christian world hold strongly to their belief that the Old Testament is archaic and not applicable to us today. They say that we must build our lives solely in the New Testament. However, Jesus and the early church wouldn't agree. In fact, the Old Testament writings were the only "Bible" the early church had. For over sixty years, the church didn't have a "Gospel" to read. It was even longer before it was widely available to the churches abroad. The only scriptures they had were the Old Testament scriptures. Don't feel sorry for them, however, because we can find most of what we read in the New Testament in the Old Testament. In fact, Jesus told the religious population:

For if you believed Moses, you would believe me; for he wrote of me.
John 5:46 (ESV)

Jesus said Moses wrote about Him? You see, the stories of the Old Testament were pictures of the coming messiah, and if you pay close attention to the details of those stories, you will see Jesus all over them.

Whenever I teach home Bible studies, we always start in the Old Testament and make our way to the New Testament. I tell the person or family that everything in the Old Testament points to the New Testament, and one of my favorite things to do when teaching a home Bible study is to go through the Old Testament and see the many stories and principles that point directly to Jesus and His Gospel.

You see, the Old Testament is not out of date. It's still cutting edge and anointed in God-breathed words, and they point directly to Jesus and to His plan of salvation for the church. Join me on this journey through some of the Old Testament stories as we look to history to learn more about His story.

An Old Message for a New Generation

It's common practice to start at the beginning. One doesn't read a book from back to the front; nor does one watch a film in reverse. Elementary teachers don't teach their students the most complicated forms of math first, then digress into simpler ideas.

A math student must first grasp the idea of addition and subtraction fully before moving to multiplication and division. A student must first learn how to count how many apples he has left after Jerry takes two, before he can solve more complex equations with unknown variables.

When climbing a ladder, you must start at the bottom and work your way up. It's the same with the Bible. There are voluminous benefits to starting at the beginning of God's beautiful and unparalleled story.

I want to say that looking to the Old Testament for confirmation isn't a new practice, nor is it something that unbiblical. Jesus and His disciples did this frequently. For example, when Jesus would teach, He'd often point back to the Old Testament to provide more clarity on what He was teaching. Jesus quoted the Old Testament seventy-eight times in the Gospels, the Apostles quoted from the Old Testament over two hundred times in their writings.

The point is this: the Old Testament isn't in competition with the New Testament. They don't oppose one another, but the Old Testament and the New Testament both tell the same story.

Jesus, the Messiah, the Lamb of God, the Word of God made flesh. He's the one the prophets foretold. Scholars conclude conservatively that Jesus fulfilled at least three hundred

Old Testament prophecies, while some scholars say that Jesus has fulfilled over five hundred Old Testament prophecies. Either way, it's extremely clear that the history of the Bible pointed to Jesus. The entire Bible is focused on Him and on His Gospel.

Jesus came preaching His message of salvation, but it wasn't a new message. It was an old message, just presented in a new way. Jesus took old stories and revealed new principles that had always been there. So must we also start at the beginning to help us understand more about God and what His will for us is?

Jesus used the Old Testament to describe His resurrection:

For just as Jonah was three days and three nights in the belly of the great fish, so will the Son of Man be three days and three nights in the heart of the earth.

Matthew 12:40 (ESV)

Jesus pointed to Noah and Lot to describe His second coming,

Just as it was in the days of Noah, so will it be in the days of the Son of Man. They were eating and drinking and marrying and being given in marriage, until the day when Noah entered the ark, and the flood came and destroyed them all. Likewise, just as it was in the days of Lot—they were eating and drinking, buying and selling, planting and building, but on the day when Lot went out from Sodom, fire and sulfur rained from heaven and destroyed them all so will it be on the day when the Son of Man is revealed.

Luke 17:26–30 (ESV)

Jesus also uses Moses and the prophets to reveal Himself after the resurrection.

And he said to them, "O foolish ones, and slow of heart to believe all that the prophets have spoken! Was it not necessary that the Christ should suffer these things and enter into his glory?" <u>And beginning with Moses and all the Prophets, he interpreted to them in all the Scriptures the things concerning himself.</u>
Luke 24:25–27 (ESV)

Oh, how I wish I could know everything Jesus said that day, when He began with Moses and showed them it was all about Him. It wasn't about Moses; it was about Jesus. It wasn't about Jonah; it was about Jesus. It wasn't about the prophets; it was always about Jesus. The Gospel wasn't altogether a new message. Sure, it was new in the fact that it gave them new life and new purpose. But they had preached the message for thousands of years before Christ. Everything was pointing to this saving Gospel.

We find the New Testament sermons and teachings from Jesus and His apostles all throughout the Old Testament.

I pray you will walk with me for the rest of this chapter as we go back in time to revisit some old stories to see what new treasures they can offer us.

Noah

The wicked and unrighteous world, on a collision course with the impending judgement of God. Man's heart was on wicked continually, so much so that God repented that He had made man. God decided to destroy all life on earth, except for one man who found grace in the eyes of God.

The Bible says Noah "found" grace. To find something, you must look for it. Noah didn't just stumble upon grace, but the grace of God was something Noah had been searching for. He was looking for God's favor. God promised us that if we seek after Him with all our hearts, we shall find Him (Jeremiah 29:13).

Noah was a righteous man, a man who loved the Lord and walked in His ways, and because of that, God gave him favor and warned Noah of the coming judgement. Not only warned, but gave him a way of escape. It was a plan of salvation for Noah and his family.

Noah, I am going to destroy the earth with water; but since you found favor with me, I'm giving you the chance to choose salvation. If you want to be saved, you must build a boat. You must build with this type of wood, build it with this number of doors and windows, build it with three levels, and build it to this exact size. Pitch it inside and out. Noah, I am giving you the option to save your family. This is what you must do.

Notice how God didn't force salvation on Noah? God's grace gave Noah a plan, but Noah's salvation depended on if he followed the plan. God's grace made Noah's salvation possible, but Noah's obedience completed it.

It's important to understand that God didn't give Noah options. God didn't give Noah several ways he could be saved. God gave Noah only one option; because there's only one way out of destruction: God's way. This is a picture of Jesus Christ, who in the New Testament declared these words:

Jesus said to him, "I am the way, and the truth, and the life. No one comes to the Father except through me."

John 14:6 (ESV)

Jesus didn't give options. He declared Himself to be the only option. Jesus made many angry because of His bold statements, and the religious population of that day didn't like that. They didn't like that Jesus was claiming to be the only way. They didn't like that Jesus said there were many wrong ways, but only one right way.

The world has many roads that all end at different destinations, and with Rome being the capital of innovation during that time, it was said that all roads led to Rome. Jesus came against that, because all roads may lead to Rome, but only one road leads to the Father.

The apparent truth is this: Noah could have built a different boat, with a unique design, with different material, and, on a normal occasion, it probably would've floated. But not on that occasion, because it was God's flood, and the only way out was on God's boat. If Noah would've disobeyed, they wouldn't have survived the flood. So, the first point is this: His way is the only way. There's only one way to be saved, and that's God's way.

Second, Noah's story foreshadows water baptism. It was ultimately God who saved them, but He did so using water. God's plan that took them through the water saved Noah's family. The Apostle Peter teaches this in His first letter:

Because they formerly did not obey, when God's patience waited in the days of Noah, while the ark was being prepared, in which

> *a few, that is, eight persons, were brought safely through water. Baptism, which corresponds to this, now saves you, not as a removal of dirt from the body but as an appeal to God for a good conscience, through the resurrection of Jesus Christ.*
>
> **1 Peter 3:20–21 (ESV)**

The principle of water baptism wasn't first introduced by John the Baptist, God introduced it only ten generations from Adam and Eve. History really is His-story.

The Apostle was clear, just like water saved Noah's family, so also does baptism save us. Water baptism is an essential part of God's New Testament boat.

Moses

The story of Moses, easily one of my personal favorites. The Hebrew boy born to die in the Nile River, but saved by the mercy of an Egyptian princess. Born as a slave to Egypt, yet raised as a prince of Egypt. Born as a lesser citizen, only to be raised in the highest courts of the kingdom.

Moses's early life is a startlingly vivid picture of the favor of God. A baby that shouldn't have lived long enough to support the weight of his own head grows to support the weight of an entire nation. Spared by the grace and plan of God. He was delivered from danger so he could deliver others from the same dangers. There's a message in that as well, the purpose of our deliverance is to deliver others. The purpose of our salvation is to help save others. However, that isn't my intention here. Instead, I want to show you how Moses and his story reveal Jesus and the New Testament plan of salvation. Repentance, water baptism, and the infilling of the Holy Spirit.

Moses was special. He was an Israelite. Born to his mother, Jochebed, during a time where Hebrew boys were commanded to be killed. However, Jochebed hides her baby from the soldiers. She hides him until she can no longer do so safely, and eventually she builds a small ark and places her baby in the river, hidden among the weeds.

Once again, God's plan begins with an ark in the water. His sister Miriam stays close to watch and makes sure the baby remains safe. After all, Pharaoh wants the child dead. The name Miriam is the Hebrew form of Mary, so we see this parallel. Pharaoh is killing all the baby boys and Miriam is watching over Moses, in the same way that King Herod orders the death of all male children in Bethlehem under the age of two, and Mary watches over baby Jesus.

Coincidentally, Mary and Joseph flee to Egypt and live there until it's safe to return, meaning Jesus spent His earliest years in Egypt. The story of Moses, in many ways, is an image of the story of Jesus.

Moses is found by Pharaoh's daughter, and she has compassion for the child and adopts him, thus saving him from his fate in the river. The Egyptian princess raises Moses; he has access to the best of everything society offered. Nevertheless, when he comes of age, Moses chooses to be counted among the people of God, rather than enjoy the pleasures of sin and Egypt (Hebrews 11:24–26).

There are a few events that happen which push Moses out of Egypt, and he becomes labeled as a fugitive. After many years of Moses living in the land of Midian, he has a supernatural encounter with the Lord. Please forgive me for paraphrasing such a large portion of the story.

During the encounter, Moses was called by God to deliver God's people out of bondage. To go back to Egypt and to bring Israel out of slavery. God promises them a land; a land that "flows with milk and honey." Israel is enslaved to Egypt; they had been for four hundred years. God has promised them deliverance, and He has promised them a future in their "Promise Land."

Pharaoh doesn't immediately let them go, but with ten plagues of persuasion, Pharaoh finally relents and releases Israel to leave. On that last night, however, before the tenth plague, God warns His people of what this plague would bring.

A death angel would come through the land of Egypt during the night and would take the life of every firstborn in Egypt, including any firstborn of the Israelites, unless they followed God's instructions. God gives them instructions for their salvation; more specifically, the salvation of their firstborns, we'll talk more about this in chapter 6 "Kingdom of the Second Born."

Everything that God tells His people to do on that last night was to save their firstborn. They must kill a lamb and apply the blood to their doorpost, and when the angel comes in the night, any house with the blood applied, judgement would pass over and they would spare the home. An extraordinary picture of New Testament salvation and the blood of Jesus Christ. When judgement comes to you, to collect the penalty of your sins, only the blood of Jesus can save you.

When the angel came, it passed over the homes with the blood. The blood of a lamb spared Israel that day. From that time forward, even until today, the Jewish people have celebrated the feast of Passover, a time to commemorate the day they applied the blood and received mercy. When Jesus is crucified and gives His blood for us, it's during Passover, chronologically connecting the blood of a lamb in the Old Testament to the blood of the Lamb in the New Testament. History is His-story.

So, they are spared, and mercy is shown to Israel. In the morning, they leave Egypt with great joy, removing themselves from bondage. Slavery is in their rearview mirror, and the promise land is in their GPS. After they've left and separated themselves from Egypt, Pharaoh changes his mind and chases after Israel to overtake them and bring them back. When you choose to leave Egypt and leave the bondage of sin, hell won't let you go easily. Egypt chases Israel all the way to the Red Sea, and traps Israel.

Egypt behind them and the Red Sea in front of them. All hope seems lost until Moses prays. Once again, the Lord gives instructions. Moses stretches his rod over the sea and God parts the Red Sea, allowing Moses and the children of Israel to pass through on dry ground. Once they get to the other side, they're safe. The Egyptian army has drowned, and Israel is safely on the other side.

They begin their journey through the wilderness to reach their destination, with God leading them every step of the way. With a pillar of cloud by day and a pillar of fire by night. The Spirit of God would come down as a cloud and they'd hear God speak from the cloud. The entire episode is, step by step, a representation of the New Testament plan of salvation that came through Jesus Christ.

Israel leaving Egypt is a picture of repentance, turning away from sin and leaving the thing that bound you. Going through the waters of the Red Sea is a picture of water baptism. Repentance isn't enough because hell will still chase after you, but it's the waters of baptism that wash away your sin in the same way the waters of the red sea washed away Egypt's army.

Then, after the water, the cloud of God's Spirit filled their camps, rested on the mountain, and later filled the tabernacle. After they came through the water, God would baptize their camps with His Spirit. After water baptism came the Spirit baptism. The entire story is a picture of what was to come.

If you think I'm stretching to make this correlation, let's look at what Paul wrote:

For I do not want you to be unaware, brothers, that our fathers were all under the cloud, and all passed through the sea, and all were baptized into Moses in the cloud and in the sea,

1 Corinthians 10:1–2 (ESV)

Paul used this story in the same way to teach water baptism and Spirit baptism. It's important to note that Paul said *all* were under the cloud, *all* passed through the sea, and *all* were baptized. The same thing happened on the day of Pentecost.

And they were ALL filled with the Holy Spirit and began to speak in other tongues as the Spirit gave them utterance.

Acts 2:4 (ESV)

See, this isn't only for a few, but this is for everybody. These are God's instructions on how we get to our promise land; this is God's plan to get His church ready for heaven. Repentance, water baptism and Spirit baptism. Moses testifies to this truth. History is His-story.

The Tabernacle of Moses

In the wilderness, camped at the base of Mount Sinai, Moses follows the calling of God to hike to the top of the mount. There, at the top, Moses encounters God. And for forty days and nights, God speaks with Moses.

It's during this time that Moses receives the Ten Commandments and the instructions to build a sanctuary for the Lord. For seven chapters, Exodus 25–32, God gives Moses precise instructions on how he must build the tabernacle. First, God gives Moses the purpose of why he must build the tabernacle.

And let them make me a sanctuary, that I may dwell in their midst.
Exodus 25:8 (ESV)

The entire purpose of building this tabernacle was to provide a place for God's presence to dwell. God wanted, and still wants, to be in the middle of His people. But because of sin, a barrier separated man from God. Man didn't have free access to God, therefore the Lord had to come up with a plan that would allow man access to Him. A process that would prepare sinful men to come into the presence of a holy and sinless God.

That was the church of the Old Testament, where the people came to pray and worship, where they'd bring their sacrifices.

That was the physical location of the Spirit of God: a wilderness sanctuary. A beautiful and spiritual oasis in the middle of a desert. A picture of the church in the world, a place of peace in a world of chaos. And much like Noah's ark, the tabernacle plan was extremely precise. And God was clear that they must carry out the plans exactly as He commanded them to be carried out.

Exactly as I show you concerning the pattern of the tabernacle, and of all its furniture, so you shall make it.

Exodus 25:9 (ESV)

He then follows with detailed instructions for every part of the tabernacle. God told them what pieces of furniture to build and what size to build them. The type of wood that needed to be used, what type of metal needed to encase it. The number of rings they had to attach to each piece of furniture.

Even the walls of the tabernacle were in the plans. The animal skins that needed to be used, multiple types they would layer in a particular order. The oil used in the lamps had to be made with certain ingredients. The priests had a dress code, certain things they had to wear to walk through the tabernacle. Everything was exact, and it wasn't man's plan, it was God's plan.

God's way is not a mystery, but it's a clear path that's marked with explicit instructions. God's way will always work if we do it His way. God's plan must be followed God's way.

All this detailed effort, all because God wanted man to have access to Him. We must never forget God's desire is us. It always has been, always will be. The first point, however, is the fact that this plan was very detailed, and God was serious about the people executing His plan, His way. We must find God's plan and follow it God's way.

I wrote about this tabernacle because it's a beautiful picture of the New Testament salvation. The layout of this wilderness sanctuary was as follows; three main sections: the outer court, the inner court or the Holy Place, and the Holy of Holies or the Most Holy Place. See diagram*

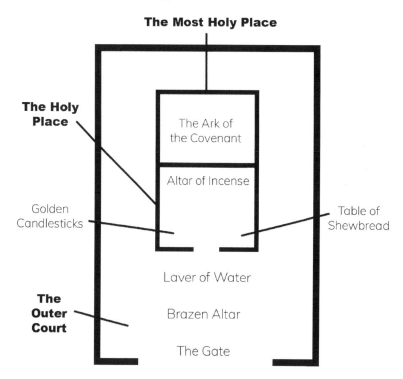

They laid the tabernacle out in that order. You'd enter the gate from the east, as the entrance into the tabernacle faced east. Interestingly enough, the entrance to the Garden of Eden also faced the east (see Gen. 3:24).

There was only one entrance to Moses's tabernacle, one gate that allowed access to God's Sanctuary. There was only one door to Noah's ark of safety. There was only one entrance into the boat that would save from God's coming judgement. In the tabernacle, you couldn't enter how you wanted to enter, but you must enter God's way; through the gate on the east side of the structure. To bring your sacrifice and burn it on the brazen altar, you had to enter by the gate. Jesus names Himself as the entrance and only gate to salvation,

I am the door. If anyone enters by me, he will be saved and will go in and out and find pasture.

John 10:9 (ESV)

Jesus is the only door by which to enter the salvation of the New Covenant. In another place Jesus said, no man can come to the Father but by Him. Jesus didn't give options. He didn't identify multiple doors, but He said, "I am the door." Noah's Ark had one door, the tabernacle had one door, and New Testament salvation only has one door. That door is Jesus.

After you enter the gate, the first piece of furniture you reach is the brazen altar. The largest piece of all the furniture. It was where the animal sacrifice were placed and burned for the sins of the people. Its entire purpose was to atone for the sins of a man and his family temporarily. When their sins demanded their blood, they brought another blood.

It wasn't a perfect substitute, however, because the blood of goats and bulls wasn't strong enough to cover their sins. Human sin demanded a human's blood. Humanity was enslaved by their sin. Trapped in an endless cycle of sacrificing lambs and calves, every year bringing another innocent animal to push back the ever-increasing debt they owed to sin.

So much time, effort, and blood, all for a temporary solution. Until the day God came and provided Himself to be a sacrifice. When sin demanded our blood, Jesus gave His own blood. Thus, God purchased the church with His own blood according to the Book of Acts. In doing so, God paid the debt we rightfully owe. Not with money or currency, but with His blood.

Neither by the blood of goats and calves, but by his own blood he entered in once into the holy place, having obtained eternal redemption for us. For if the blood of bulls and of goats, and the ashes of an heifer sprinkling the unclean, sanctifieth to the purifying of the flesh: How much more shall the blood of Christ, who through the eternal Spirit offered himself without spot to God, purge your conscience from dead works to serve the living God?
Hebrews 9:12–14 (KJV)

Every part of the tabernacle points to Jesus in such powerful ways. However, for the purpose of this book, we'll only focus on the outer court. The first step in performing duties in the tabernacle was the altar of sacrifice. After offering the sacrifice on the altar, the next step would be the brazen laver of water in which the priest would cleanse himself, washing himself with water in preparation to go into the Holy Place. After the laver and washing of water, the priest would then change his clothes, putting on the correct garments, then he would pour oil over his head. Then and only then could he enter the Holy Place.

This is a step-by-step picture of the New Testament plan of salvation. Step one is the brazen altar, the altar where the request would be made to God for forgiveness of sins. This is a picture of New Testament repentance. Next is the laver of water and the washing of the body with the water. This is a stark picture of New Testament baptism.

Following the water would be the changing of the garments and the oil poured over the priest's head. This points directly to the infilling of the Holy Ghost. The first three steps of the tabernacle are a picture of the first three components of New Testament salvation. To enter the tabernacle's Holy Place, one had to enter the gate, visit the altar, be washed by water, and covered by oil.

In the New Testament there's only one way to enter the Holy Places of God, you must first enter through Jesus, then visit the altar of repentance, have your sins washed away in the waters of baptism, and have the Holy Spirit fill and anoint you, letting Him change you inside and out. This is the only way. This is God's way.

Jesus used Moses to preach about Himself, and the writer of Hebrews says Jesus came by "a greater and more perfect tabernacle." I love how history testifies of His-Story. Everything in the Word of God points to Jesus. He is the centerpiece of scripture. Choose His way, choose His plan.

Conclusion

This chapter has explored a few stories and characters of the Old Testament that were, in fact, a picture of what was to come. We could have visited many more stories to uncover more types and shadows of Jesus and His salvation. Time fails me to talk about how Abraham unknowingly prophesied on Moriah to his son Isaac. When his son asked about the sacrifice, Abraham responded with this:

> *And Abraham said, My son, God will provide himself a lamb for a burnt offering: so they went both of them together.*
>
> **Genesis 22:8 (KJV)**

I'm not sure that Abraham had full knowledge of what that meant. I sometimes wonder if he somehow knew that one day God would literally provide Himself a lamb. Not just for the saving of one, but to provide salvation for all.

When no man or woman was good enough or strong enough to defeat sin, God Himself came. When man couldn't, God did. He didn't have to. He doesn't owe us anything, but oh how much we owe Him. Propelled by His unyielding love for us, He left the comforts of heaven to live on a cursed and sin torn earth. He bore our griefs and felt our shame. He came to bind the brokenhearted and to preach deliverance to those held captive by sin. He was bruised and beaten, rejected and crucified, for sins He never committed. All for this one reason, "For God so loved the world."

He came to open a door that no man had the strength to open, the door that closed when man first sinned. The door of open communion with God. I am free to walk with God just as Adam did before the fall. History will always be His story, and I want my story to be His story.

5
History is His-Story
Part 2

Receiving the end of your faith, even the salvation of your souls. Of which salvation the prophets have enquired and searched diligently...

—The Apostle Peter

In this chapter, I'll attempt to build on the focus of the previous chapter. It's my desire that with the help of a few more stories and characters, I may strengthen this one biblical fact: New Testament salvation wasn't a new idea. Quite the contrary, because centuries before Christ, the prophets of the Old Testament caught fleeting glimpses and prophesied about salvation principles they themselves didn't fully understand, nor did they have access to them.

The Apostle Peter said in his first letter that the prophets enquired and searched diligently for this new salvation construct.

Water baptism wasn't a new idea; repentance wasn't a new idea; and the infilling of the Holy Ghost wasn't a new idea; it was in God's plan from the very beginning.

It was always God's intentions to provide an escape from sin for His people. New Testament salvation, according to Jesus and His apostles, is: Repentance, water baptism in the name of Jesus, and the infilling of the Holy Spirit. And of course, continuing to follow His example and do His will. But this water and Spirit pattern is clearly pictured and written throughout the Old Testament scripture. You see this plan not in an unclear way, but in a way that is precise.

In the previous chapter, we talked about Noah, Moses, and the tabernacle. Each of those stories shows New Testament salvation beautifully; allow me to point to a few more stories and characters to help solidify this claim that history is His-story.

Joshua

Forty years of wandering in the wilderness, unable to cross the Jordan River because of their doubt that God could give them what He promised.

Fear of obstacles much bigger than them stole their focus and averted their attention. Taking their eyes off the promise and placing them on the problem. The problem, of course, was the giants. The giants living in the land God was going to give them.

Darkened by the shadow of giant-sized fear, the people of Israel turned their backs to God, and with their faces toward Egypt, they shouted for new leadership. They threatened to stone Moses and Aaron; that's when God stepped in and interrupted the chaos.

God was angry. After all He did for the people; delivering them; saving them; protecting them; feeding them; watering them, and healing them. They would turn and threaten to murder the man of God and the priest for the people? God was ready to destroy them, but Moses stepped in.

Moses stood between the anger of a holy God, and the guilt of a sinful people, and Moses pleaded for God to have mercy. Moses stood in the gap for people trying to murder him! And in that we have a beautiful picture of what was to come, when Jesus would be tortured, beaten, mocked, and crucified. While hanging naked on the cross, He'd still use His last few breaths to say, "Father, forgive them."

Wrecked by pain, Jesus could still pray for those who wanted to kill Him. A powerful example of this glorious Gospel. That's what Moses does. He prays for the people that want to kill him, and God hears Moses and shows mercy. However, God passes a judgement; none of them that turned against God, can enter the Promise Land.

Banished between Egypt and Canaan. Forced by their own unfaithfulness and hostility, to wander in the wilderness for forty years. Until the last man and woman, from the generation of those who wouldn't trust God, die. And after that generation passes, God will raise in the new generation to inherit the promises of God.

Moses, unfortunately, is part of that disbelieving generation. Moses dies outside of the Promise Land. The proverbial torch Moses carried so well was handed to Joshua. That man was God's new leader, who brought Israel across the Jordan River and into their promise. After forty years of wandering, the time finally arrives. The time to go across the river and into the promise. Before crossing over, God says to Joshua,

And the LORD said unto Joshua, This day will I begin to magnify thee in the sight of all Israel, that they may know that, as I was with Moses, so I will be with thee. And thou shalt command the priests that bear the ark of the covenant, saying, When ye are come to the brink of the water of Jordan, ye shall stand still in Jordan.

Joshua 3:7–8 (KJV)

Joshua, I want to show the people I am with you just as I was with Moses. When you get to the water, command the priest to stand in the water. Joshua obeys, and this happens:

And as they that bare the ark were come unto Jordan, and the feet of the priests that bare the ark were dipped in the brim of the water, (for Jordan overfloweth all his banks all the time of harvest,) That the waters which came down from above stood and rose up upon an heap very far from the city Adam, that is beside Zaretan: and those that came down toward the sea of the plain, even the salt sea, failed, and were cut off: and the people passed over right against Jericho. And the priests that bare the ark of the covenant of the LORD stood firm on dry ground in the midst of Jordan, and all the Israelites passed over on dry ground, until all the people were passed clean over Jordan.

Joshua 3:15–17 (KJV)

In the same way that God miraculously parted the Red Sea to bring them out of Egypt, God miraculously parts the Jordan River to bring them into the Promise Land. In the same way that the passing through the Red Sea was a picture of baptism, Joshua passing through the Jordan was also a picture of baptism.

Because it was a new generation, and while the previous generation had gone through the water, the new generation hadn't. The baptism of the previous generation didn't cover the new generation. So, once again, God parted the waters to allow the people of Israel to pass through the water supernaturally.

Water baptism is for you, and it's for your children, and for their children. The new generation needed to go through the waters for themselves. It was important to God that there be a supernatural passing through the water.

The wilderness had become their place of exile. It was their place of sins and consequence. When they left the wilderness, it was a picture of repentance; they passed through the water of the Jordan river miraculously; and when they got to the promise land, the Lord entered their camp to help them fight their battles. This salvation concept of repentance, water baptism, and receiving the Spirit of God isn't a new concept. God has been using it for millennia.

Elijah

The infamous ministry of the prophet Elijah. The man who walked and talked with God. The man who carried the voice and the authority of the mighty God. His word started and ended a three-year drought. At the word of Elijah, the heavens shut, and no rain fell for three years.

The man who sat beside the brook, and who ravens fed daily by bringing him food. The man who told the widow woman who only had enough food for one more meal, "make me a cake first." He reassured her of course, telling her not to be afraid because: "God said your meal barrel would not run out." And when the woman made Elijah food, there was enough for another meal, then another, and another. Her barrel of food never ran out.

Elijah was the man who walked into the bedroom of a dead child, stretched himself over the breathless boy; and after he prayed, the boy came alive again. The man who prayed a prayer and fire fell from heaven. That's the ministry of Elijah.

The second and last person recorded in the Bible to not experience death, God came down from heaven in a chariot and took him home. Elijah's story is powerful. Full of faith and miracles, running over with boldness and authority. Elijah, the man who carried the power of God. His life was legendary. Everybody in that day knew who Elijah, the prophet of God, was.

The anointing he carried was astounding. He was no obscure figure; he was no side character in the biblical narrative. His story wasn't pointless filler, but his ministry had tremendous purpose from God. Not only for his day, but for our day as well.

Elijah was a God-sent blessing to the people of Israel during his day, and his ancient story is no less important to us today. His story beautifully shows us that God always provides for His own. When the rest of the land was in drought and famine, Elijah had a brook; Elijah had ravens to bring food, and Elijah had a widowed woman to bake for him.

But even more than that, Elijah's story shows us a glimpse into New Testament salvation. Over eight hundred years before the birth of Jesus, eight hundred years before His wondrous presentation of this New Covenant we call the Gospel. Eight hundred years before Jesus told Nicodemus all must be born again of water and of Spirit. Eight hundred years before Jesus said, "He that believes and is baptized shall be saved."

So many years before the blood of the cross; before the burial and resurrection. Before all of that, Elijah gave us a glimpse of what was to come.

It was quite possibly the climax of Elijah's story, standing on the top of Mount Carmel. Badly outnumbered by false prophets of a fake god, surrounded by an enemy that wanted him dead. Elijah, under the anointing he was carrying, challenges them.

"You build an altar to your god, and I will build an altar to my God, and the God the answers by fire, let Him be God." (1 Kings 18:24) A bold challenge accepted by the false prophets. The other prophets built an altar, and with significant effort, they called on their god. To no avail, however, because they received no response. They saw no fire. There was no gratification in their extreme display of desperate travail.

When they finished, Elijah built his altar and presented a sacrifice before his God, and in doing so, he opened the shutters of the window of time to give us a glimpse of eight hundred years in the future.

He built the altar, and on it he laid the sacrifice. Which was completely normal for his time, build the altar and lay the bloody remains of the animal carcass onto the altar. Then light a fire underneath it and let it burn before your God. But it was different. Elijah did something brand new, something unheard of. Elijah said, "bring me four buckets of water," and he took the water and he dumped it over the sacrifice.

He did that three times, dumping twelve buckets of water onto the blood-soaked remains of the bull; and after a single, brief prayer, the fire of God falls and consumes the sacrifice and the water. Thus proving to everyone there that the Lord God of Elijah was the one true God.

But what is special about this story is what Elijah did that's new. Nobody used water in their sacrifice. Elijah built the altar; provided the blood; then Elijah baptized the sacrifice with water and God responded by baptizing the sacrifice with fire. A clear picture of the blood, water, and Spirit pattern. The blood of repentance, the water of baptism, and the fire of the Holy Spirit.

Normally they'd light their own fire to burn the sacrifice, but when Elijah baptized his sacrifice with water, God baptized with fire: and in the same way, if we will repent of our sins, are baptized in water in the name of Jesus, then God will answer by fire. He'll fill us with the gift of the Holy Ghost.

Just as the cloven tongues of fire fell on the apostles in Acts chapter two, the fire can fall on you and on your family. All Elijah did was present repentance and water baptism, and God did the rest to prove His glory.

In this hour, full of false teachings and false doctrines. May we present repentance and water baptism, and watch as God gives our cities the fire of the Holy Ghost.

Ezekiel

Ezekiel, the prophet in exile. The mouthpiece of God for a people who had forsaken Him. The clear proof God loves and cares for His people no matter what unfortunate and dire situation they've gotten themselves into.

When the nation of Israel broke their covenants with God, bringing idols into the temple, worshiping false gods instead of the one true God. The god-saturated nation of Babylon came in and took the people of Jerusalem into captivity. Dragging them away from their homeland and depositing them into a strange culture.

Remember, this wasn't God's fault, it was theirs entirely. But even though they were no longer in Jerusalem, the city of God's people, God was still with them. He didn't let them go into exile alone, but followed them into the new season. And there in Babylon, God anointed a prophet to the people. He chose a man to speak His words, and to remind Israel of the promises He had given to them and to their fathers.

In that new and uncomfortable place, God reminded them of the new covenant He had prepared for them in their future. It was a completely new relational dynamic they could experience with their Creator. God had always been with them, but it was never enough because there were many things, good and bad, that were with them consistently. God with them wasn't enough to keep them out of the deadly distractions of idolatry and the darkness of sin.

Every day, they had to fight the outward and inward battles of sin and temptation, and they were always losing the battle. But in exile, God used Ezekiel to remind the people of God that one day soon, everything would change. It would no longer be God *with* them, but it will be God *in* them.

In such a beautiful way, God once again laid out the exact pattern He gave to Moses. He gave them a blood, water, and Spirit pattern. Read what God spoke through the Prophet Ezekiel:

I will sprinkle clean water on you, and you shall be clean from all your uncleannesses, and from all your idols I will cleanse you. And I will give you a new heart, and a new spirit I will put within you. And I will remove the heart of stone from your flesh and give you a heart of flesh. And I will put my Spirit within you, and cause you to walk in my statutes and be careful to obey my rules.

Ezekiel 36:25–27 (ESV)

Another marvelous picture of the New Covenant, over five hundred years before the birth of Christ! God spoke through Ezekiel the wonderful truths of the glorious Gospel of Jesus Christ. The one who would come to save us from our sins. He'd fight the battle we could never win, to get victory over an enemy we were never strong enough to defeat.

He'd tear down the wall of unholy sin that separated us from the holiness of God, allowing His Spirit to come and live inside of us. It was a new covenant, but it wasn't a new idea. All biblical history pointed to Jesus and His message.

God spoke the message of repentance in receiving a new heart; the message of cleansing by water, foreshadowing the water baptism of the New Testament; and the message of receiving the Spirit of God into our bodies, which in the New Testament language is receiving the gift of the Holy Ghost through Ezekiel.

The evident truth is this: repentance, water baptism, and the infilling of the Holy Ghost were always the plan! Set Ezekiel's message alongside the apostle Peter's message, and see if there is anything different.

I will sprinkle clean water on you, and you shall be clean from all your uncleannesses, and from all your idols I will cleanse you. And I will give you a new heart, and a new spirit I will put within you. And I will remove the heart of stone from your flesh and give you a heart of flesh. And I will put my Spirit within you, and cause you to walk in my statutes and be careful to obey my rules.

Ezekiel 36:25–27 (ESV)

Now when they heard this they were cut to the heart, and said to Peter and the rest of the apostles, "Brothers, what shall we do?" And Peter said to them, "Repent and be baptized every one of you in the name of Jesus Christ for the forgiveness of your sins, and you will receive the gift of the Holy Spirit."

Acts 2:37–38 (ESV)

They are the same message! This was always the redemptive plan of God. So why should we change it now? God showed it to Noah, Moses, and those who came into the tabernacle. He showed it to Joshua and Isaiah. He showed it to David and Ezekiel. And finally, it culminated and came to fruition in the New Testament with the apostles and the birth of the church.

God's message is perfect. It doesn't need us to fix it. God's plan is better than our plan. Quit trying to change it. Let God be true, and every man a liar. If you haven't repented of your sins and let God give you a new heart, then do it. Because there's nothing more beautiful to see when someone lets God change them for the better.

If you haven't been water baptized in the name of Jesus, then do it because God wants to cleanse you and wash you of the stains of sin. If you haven't been filled with the Holy Ghost, then find a church that believes in biblical New Testament salvation, and go receive the gift of the Holy Ghost. This isn't a new thing, this is everything. History screams these truths. It's the message of Jesus Christ. History is His-Story.

Conclusion

We know we have God; He is always with us. He never leaves us nor forsakes us, and I will forever rejoice in that fact. He has already pledged Himself to us. You can never run far enough to escape His reach. You can never fall low enough to over-extend His arm. You can never be so lost that He can't find you. You can never be in a darkness black enough to block His light. Nothing can separate you from the love of God.

Every night you lay your head on your pillow to sleep, it's God who keeps your heart beating, your blood pumping, your lungs breathing, and your kidneys filtering. All night long, every system in your body continues to function because God doesn't leave you. God is there when you're sleeping and He's there when you're walking. He's there in the good and in the bad. I'm so thankful we always have God.

Whether or not we have God isn't the question, we undoubtably have God. But the all-important question is this: does God have you? Have you given Him your sin hardened heart? Have you let Him wash you with water and revive you with His Spirit? Have you let Him give you a new life? God is always with us because He is a faithful God. But God WITH us doesn't save us, God IN us is what saves us.

"To them God chose to make known how great among the Gentiles are the riches of the glory of this mystery, which is Christ in you, the hope of glory."

Colossians 1:27 (ESV)

"Little children, you are from God and have overcome them, for he who is in you is greater than he who is in the world."

1 John 4:4 (ESV)

You can't make it without Him. You cannot beat sin without Him. You cannot beat addiction without Him. You cannot beat depression without Him. You cannot be saved without Him. But if you obey His Gospel, and let God live inside you, you can win. It's Christ in you, the hope of glory.

Make this next statement your reality, "He that is IN me, is greater…."

6
Kingdom of the Second-Born

"Marvel not that I said unto you, You must be born again."

—Jesus

I am not living for the kingdoms of this world. Jesus told us to "seek first the kingdom of God and His righteousness." We must never forget that everything we know down here is temporary and, like Abraham, we're looking for a city whose builder and maker are God. The lyrics to the timeless hymn say this:

> *This world is not our home, we are just passing through, our treasures are laid up, somewhere beyond the blue, the angels beckon me, from heavens open door, and I can't feel at home in this world anymore.*

We are being called to a kingdom that never ends, a home far above the clouds, where we'll forever be with our loving savior.

David wrote a beautiful poem about God making him to lie down in green pastures and still waters, and that sounds amazing.

I'm thankful for the beautiful moments of life that God allows us to experience. The seasons of green pastures and still waters. However, may we never become so enthralled with the green pastures of this life that we forget about the golden streets of the next life. May we never become so attached to the peacefully still waters of our greatest memories here that we take our focus off the river of life in Heaven.

Oh, how I want to go to heaven. Jesus promised me He was going to prepare a place for me, and above all else, I want that place. There's no place on earth that can compare to the place God has made specifically for you.

You can't devise a plan as great as God's plan. You'll never find a better image for your life than God's image for your life. The most beautiful and spectacular wonders of this modern world are a fleeting shadow compared to His kingdom.

The wonders of the ancient world have powerfully risen and pitifully fallen, but God's kingdom has never and will never fall. We remember Rome from its ruins and we remember Babylon from the stories told, but heaven has no ruins and heaven's stories have yet to be told.

The empires; kingdoms; and governments of today are becoming increasingly stained with sin and evil, but God has a kingdom that is free from hurt and misery. A city beyond the clouds, without disease and cancer. There will be no fighting there, no pain or struggles to bear. May we, as Abraham of old, look for a city with foundations whose builder and maker is God.

I'm so extremely blessed to be a citizen of the United States of America. May we never take for granted the blessed freedoms we enjoy. Nevertheless, my premiere citizenship is God's kingdom. I am a citizen of heaven first, and a citizen of America second.

Heaven is the most glorious place in the universe. No eye has seen, nor ear heard, neither has any heart imagined the things God has prepared for those that love Him.

I could go on with my feeble attempts at using adjectives to paint a picture of heaven for you, but the truth is that heaven is much greater than the greatest song lyric, or heaven poem you may find. Let me stop trying to describe it, and get right to the point: God has a kingdom, and it's for you. I don't care what your life story is, Jesus has prepared a place for you. The most important question in life is this; how can I join His kingdom?

The answer is actually quite simple; it's not a dark mystery or complicated equation. The only way to enter His kingdom is to be born again. It's surprising how quick Jesus gives this answer, when Nicodemus came to Him with questions regarding the kingdom. One would think Jesus might lean into His answer slowly, or maybe carefully lead up to His answer. However, Jesus does neither; he promptly answers with a clean cut response.

Jesus answered and said unto him, Verily, verily, I say unto thee, Except a man be born again, he cannot see the kingdom of God.

John 3:3 (KJV)

And that was it. They aren't my words, or any other preacher's words. This was Jesus's quick and sure response, "except a man be born again he cannot see the kingdom of God"

Nicodemus is taken aback, confused, and with a bewildering tone he asks "how?" It's very certain Jesus has put significant emphasis on our birth. We're not simply granted access to this kingdom, we are born into this kingdom.

Even though the response from Jesus was absolute, "be born again," I'd like to point out that, once again, it wasn't a new idea. While it's true that Jesus didn't take any time to lead up to His response to Nicodemus, He definitely took time to lead up to this idea of a second birth. Thousands of years before this conversation between Jesus and Nicodemus, God was already giving us an idea of what was to come. The stories of the Old Testament clearly show that God's kingdom wouldn't follow the ordinary pattern of birthright.

Your birthright comes from your birth. When you are born, you receive a name. It's the name your family gives you, and whatever family you're born into, or adopted by, you take their name. I was born into the Jones family; therefore, I inherited the Jones name. And by that birthright, I grew up living in the Jones home, and eating from the Jones table.

My dad is a preacher, and I became a preacher. My dad also owned a construction company for most of my life, and I now have my own construction company. My mother plays the piano, and I also play the piano.

All of this, I was blessed to inherit because I was born into this family. My attitude, temperament, hair color, and height can all point back to my birth. And in the same way, Jesus said to live in His kingdom, we must be "born again" into His kingdom. But the question is, how?

I've already been born, and it certainly wasn't into the kingdom of God. It was into a sin sickened world. No matter how great I may feel the Jones name is, it will never be great enough to grant me access into heaven. My birthright as a Jones may have blessed me with many things, but in the view of an eternity, it's severely lacking. Your first birth will never be good enough to save you. Which is why Jesus said you must be born again.

Your first birth was natural, but Jesus said you must be born spiritually. You were born into sin with your first birth, but you're born out of sin when you're born again. Here's a beautiful point about the Gospel of Jesus. Your first birth is irrelevant.

It doesn't matter what your family background is, and it doesn't matter what name you inherited with your first birth. You can never be born rich enough to save yourself, and you can never be born poor enough to discount yourself. It doesn't matter if you have a good name, a bad name, or no name. To be a part of God's kingdom, you must have a new name and a new birth. It's not about the name you were born with, it's all about the name that you were born again with.

The child born into an upper-class family and the child born in the homeless shelter are on equal ground in the eyes of God. Both need to be born again. The child born with loving parents and the newborn orphan must one day be born again. So here's the point of all of that: the Kingdom of God is for the second born.

The Plan from the Beginning.

In ancient history, it was customary that the larger portion of the inheritance belonged to the first-born. The family home, the family business, and the more important matters of the family lifestyle would pass down to the first-born son. Even in royal families, it was normally the first-born son that was next in line for the kingship.

The first-born was the eldest, and because of that, he'd receive the blessing and position as head of the family. But God has always operated differently than the world operates and for that, I am thankful. The systems of this world are flawed, but God's systems are perfect.

God doesn't make it up as He goes, but from the very beginning, God has had a plan. From the first verse of Genesis, God knew that one day He'd set up His kingdom on earth as the New Testament Church.

Throughout the Old Testament, we see God put special emphasis on the second birth. They showed it in the very first family when Adam and Eve gave birth to Cain and Abel. Cain being the eldest and Abel being the second born. Their story on paper is quick to show us that God rejected Cain, the firstborn, and accepted Abel, the second born.

I know the reason for God's approval and disapproval wasn't their birth order, however; the principle is there. Cain kills Abel, giving us a glimpse, from the beginning of time, the fight between the first birth and the second birth. This observation would be a stretch if it ended there. However, it doesn't. Throughout the scriptures, you see this idea sewn into the story.

Let's open the shutters of scripture to take a few glances into Old Testament stories. Stories that provide insight into God's intentions of building a kingdom with the second born.

God's Promise + God's Plan

Abraham, the man who left everything, everything that was comfortable in his life, to follow the voice of God. The voice that called him from the familiar landscape of his raising and pointed him toward a new and unknown land. God didn't give Abraham a detailed step-by-step plan, instead, He gives Abraham a promise.

> *Now the Lord said to Abram, "Go from your country and your kindred and your father's house to the land that I will show you. And I will make of you a great nation, and I will bless you and make your name great, so that you will be a blessing. I will bless those who bless you, and him who dishonors you I will curse, and in you all the families of the earth shall be blessed." So Abram went, as the Lord had told him, and Lot went with him. Abram was seventy-five years old when he departed from Haran.*
>
> **Genesis 12:1–4 (ESV)**

God doesn't always give us the plan, but He always gives us the promise. We may not always know how it will work out, but we know this; if God is in it, it will undoubtedly work out. He gives us this promise in Deuteronomy 31: "It is the Lord who goes before you. He will be with you; he will not leave you or forsake you. Do not fear or be dismayed." We may not always be certain of the plan, but may we never doubt the promise.

Abraham is called away from his country, at the silvered age of seventy-five. He isn't given a detailed plan, but he receives a beautiful promise. Let me say this before moving on: just because God hasn't shown you the plan, doesn't mean that God doesn't have a plan. God always has a plan.

Abraham, if you will trust me, and follow me, I will bless you and make of you a nation. God's plan for Abraham wasn't a small plan. It was a nation-sized plan. God didn't promise Abraham a quiet and quaint life with a few family members. God promises Abraham a nation.

The problem, however, is this: at seventy-five, Abraham has no children. One cannot build a family, much less a nation, without children. God is calling a people for His name, and He chooses a seventy-five-year-old man with no children. God's ways don't always make sense because they are much higher than ours.

Abraham and his wife Sarah receive a promise. Sarah will be healed, and you will have children. Being full of faith, Abraham believes the word of God, and joyfully receives the promise; but when eleven years pass and there's still no child, they become confused. And in their clouded confusion, they decide Abraham needs a relationship with Hagar, the handmaid, and have a child with her.

In this season of weakened faith and strengthened doubt, Abraham has a child with Hagar, the servant. At eighty-six, Abraham gleefully welcomes his firstborn son into their world. They named him Ishmael. God isn't pleased with this, however, because God promised a child through Sarah, not Hagar. And no matter how much Abraham loved his new son, he wasn't the promised son.

That was man's futile attempts at bringing God's promise into reality. Blinded by the impossibility of Sarah's barrenness, they conclude that if it was going to happen, it would have to happen like that. Ishmael isn't the promise child. He is the child born from the faltering faith of Sarah and Abraham; he is the result of man trying to figure out God's promises in the most logical way possible.

Because it's not logical for an eighty-year-old barren woman to suddenly conceive, so surely God wants us to follow what makes sense in our human thinking, right? God gave us the promise, and maybe He wants us to come up with the plan? But that's dangerous and faulty thinking because God's promise will only come to pass through God's plan. Your plan, my plan, or anybody else's plan will never be good enough to make God's promise come to pass.

If God gives a promise, you can be sure He already has a plan. God has given us a promise of salvation, and it's not up to us to formulate the plan. God gave the world a promise of salvation and He also gave a plan of salvation.

And this is the thinking that caused Abraham and Sarah to come up with their own plan to bring God's promise into their lives. God doesn't accept Ishmael as the heir of the promise, because God isn't building His kingdom on man's plan, but He's building His kingdom on His plan. The plan God has had since the very beginning of time.

Ishmael is born, but God speaks to Abraham and reminds him the promise would come from Sarah. And over ten years later, Sarah conceives and gives birth to Isaac. Now Abraham has two sons, but only one of them was born from faith. Ishmael the firstborn, and Isaac the second born. God speaks to Abraham and says this:

> *But God said to Abraham, "Be not displeased because of the boy and because of your slave woman. Whatever Sarah says to you, do as she tells you, for through Isaac shall your offspring be named."*
> **Genesis 21:12 (ESV)**

God says I will build my nation from Isaac. The child born from faith. The child born of the promise. The second born. Beginning to show the principle that God's people would be built from the second born. God's promise wasn't attached to the first birth, it was with the second birth. This clearly has New Testament parallels because Paul writes about this in Galatians, where he compares the child born of the slave woman and the child born of the promise. He concludes with this:

> *Now you, brothers, like Isaac, are children of promise.*
> **Galatians 4:28 (ESV)**

Like Isaac, we are children of the promise. We're the people not born from flesh only, but born of faith. If we want to be a part of God's kingdom, we must realize it begins with spiritual and faith-filled birth. Or, as Jesus said, "born again."

The Blessing of the Second Born.

This thread doesn't end with Abraham and Isaac, but continues prominently through the story of Israel's beginning. And, for the sake of time, let me hurry through these next examples.

Isaac, the promised son of Abraham, has two sons; twins. The older son being Esau, the younger being Jacob. Their birth is interesting, because during the birth, the Bible says there was a struggle in her womb. In fact, it explicitly says "The children struggled together in her womb." There are two sons, one would be born first, with the other following second. They struggled together in the womb. The Lord speaks to their mother, Rebekah, and says this:

And the Lord said to her, "Two nations are in your womb, and two peoples from within you shall be divided; the one shall be stronger than the other, the older shall serve the younger."

Genesis 25:23 (ESV)

What a strange word the Lord gave Rebekah. The second born will be stronger and rule over the firstborn. The children are born, Esau is born first, and Jacob followed. There's so much of this story that we could unpack, but once again, for the sake of time, let me get right to the foreshadowing of New Testament salvation.

Esau, in a moment of physical weakness, sells his birthright to Jacob for a bowl of soup. The younger brother purchases the birthright. And once again, the birthright is held by the second born and not the firstborn.

Jacob doesn't stop with purchasing the birthright, but when Isaac is aged and his eyesight has failed him. Isaac calls Esau, his firstborn, and he makes plans to give him the blessing of the firstborn. The promise that God began with Abraham, and passed down to Isaac, was going to be handed to Esau. Esau leaves to prepare a meal for his father. During Esau's absence,

Jacob comes into his father's room. He wears his older brother's clothes, he also wears animal skins to make him feel more like his brother. And he deceives his father into giving him the blessing of the firstborn. Jacob purchased the birthright and received the blessing. Fulfilling the word of the Lord given to Rebekah during her labor, "the elder will serve the younger."

God's blessing was once again passed down, not through the first birth, but through the second. It's always been God's intentions to build His people and His kingdom off the second born. Another beautiful picture of that moment when Nicodemus would come under the cover of night and ask about the kingdom, and Jesus would say, "Truly, truly, I say to you, unless one is born again he cannot see the kingdom of God."

Another strange occurrence happens in the life of Jacob. At the end of Jacob's life, moments before he'd pull his feet into the folds of the blankets of his bed, and give his last breath. All of Jacob's children of stand before him. Jacob blesses all of them.

Each son stands before him, and Jacob gives each one a unique blessing. The strange occurrence happens when Joseph stands before Jacob, and Jacob gives a double portion to Joseph. In doing so, he takes Joseph's two sons and gives them both a blessing.

The Bible says Joseph, in anticipation of what Jacob is about to do, positions his sons to receive the blessing. He does so intentionally, putting his firstborn son, Manasseh, on Jacob's right hand. Because the right hand blessing was symbolic, and it belonged to the firstborn. And Joseph guides his second-born son, Ephraim, to the left side of Jacob to receive the lesser portion. What Jacob does next is astounding, and it's a powerful continuation of the principle that God established with Abraham.

And Joseph took them both, Ephraim in his right hand toward Israel's left hand, and Manasseh in his left hand toward Israel's right hand, and brought them near him. And Israel stretched out his right hand and laid it on the head of Ephraim, who was the younger, and his left hand on the head of Manasseh, crossing his hands (for Manasseh was the firstborn).

Genesis 48:13–14 (ESV)

Jacob wittingly crosses his hands and places his right hand on the head of Ephraim, the second born; and placing the left hand on Manasseh, the firstborn. Joseph isn't pleased with this and tries to correct it.

When Joseph saw that his father laid his right hand on the head of Ephraim, it displeased him, and he took his father's hand to move it from Ephraim's head to Manasseh's head. And Joseph said to his father, "Not this way, my father; since this one is the firstborn, put your right hand on his head." But his father refused and said, "I know, my son, I know. He also shall become a people, and he also shall be great. Nevertheless, his younger brother shall be greater than he, and his offspring shall become a multitude of nations."

Genesis 48:17–19 (ESV)

Joseph tries to correct the obvious cultural mistake, but what Joseph didn't understand was that God was building His kingdom differently. God was setting up His kingdom by putting the blessing; the promise; and the authority on the second born. And Jacob refuses to let his hands be changed, because it wasn't an accident, it was the will of God. God's promise is built not on your first birth, but it is built on your second birth.

Conclusion

Are you willing to be born again? Are you willing to receive a new identity in Christ? Join the kingdom of the second born, join God's Kingdom. It's full of people who were born imperfect, flawed by sin, marred by evil, but the promise of God has made them brand new. They have been covered by the blood; washed by the water; and filled with the Spirit. Nicodemus, unless you are born of water and of Spirit, you cannot enter the kingdom of God.

One last example, if I may. After four hundred years of brutal slavery, trudging through the dirt and the grime of the slave camps, wearing the fresh scars on their backs from whippings and beatings, God delivers His people from Egypt. And God chooses a man named Moses. He was the second-born son to a woman named Jochebed. Moses had an older brother named Aaron, but God didn't choose Aaron. He chose Moses.

Even though He didn't talk as well as Aaron, the firstborn. Even though his stutter handicapped him and limited his speech. God bypasses the healthy firstborn for a handicapped second born. Because God is building this kingdom.

It is His people; It is His kingdom; It is His church; and it is His story. God is writing a perfect story. I'm so very thankful that my birth doesn't discount me. My mangled story cannot stop God's plan and promise for my life. God can deliver me. God can redeem me; save me. How you ask? I must be born again. I must be born of water in baptism, and I must be born of God's Spirit.

For in one Spirit we were all baptized into one body—Jews or Greeks, slaves or free—and all were made to drink of one Spirit.

1 Corinthians 12:13 (ESV)

On hearing this, they were baptized in the name of the Lord Jesus. And when Paul had laid his hands on them, the Holy Spirit came on them, and they began speaking in tongues and prophesying.

Acts 19:5–6 (ESV)

7

To Work or Not to Work.

The sinner's prayer has sent more people to Hell than all the bars in America.

—Leonard Ravenhill

The mantra of modern day Christianity; we can sum up the waving banner of the myriad denominations through this statement, "Salvation is by grace alone, through faith alone."

The followers of this "grace alone" movement look back to men like Martin Luther and John Calvin, who taught that salvation has nothing to do with our obedience.

Their battle cry rises out against anyone who says we must do something to be saved. There is a war waged against Christians who believe their salvation is inseparable from their obedience to the Word of God. The moment you mention water baptism, they raise the alarm that we're relying on works when we should rely on grace.

Their premise is this: Jesus already did the work, so all that's required of us is to believe in Jesus and His finished work, and we can spend eternity in Heaven. And while it sounds good to the ear, it doesn't match what the Bible says about salvation. It may have been Martin Luther's theology and John Calvin's theology, but it's never been God's theology.

Actually, I say it wasn't Luther's and Calvin's theology. However, the beliefs of followers of Luther and Calvin today greatly differ from their founders. Martin Luther believed baptism was a part of salvation, even writing explicitly so. John Calvin writes in his commentary on the book of John that baptism is necessary to be saved. Modern adaptations of these two reformers have taken the doctrines of Luther and Calvin began, and have stretched them even further.

Still, their reformed theology is nowhere near what is written in the Bible. If you don't agree with those last few sentences, then I ask sincerely, hear me out. Remember that our eternal salvation is the most important thing in our life. If we fail in every other area of our lives, may we not fail in our pursuit of God and His will for our lives.

This chapter begins with a lot of information and many scripture references, because I must not build eternal salvation on my opinions or on tradition; I must build it on His unfailing Word.

I must preface this chapter by saying this: when I speak of works, I'm referring directly to obeying the teachings of Christ and His apostles. I'm not referring to a works-based salvation as Catholicism teaches. We don't work for our salvation. We can never earn salvation, God freely gives it. But to say that we have no responsibility for our salvation? That is what's in question. Does how we live matter? Does what we do matter?

When I speak of works, I'm not talking about trying to be good enough for salvation. I'm simply contending for obedience to His word. Remember, let God be true and every man a liar.

To be or not to be

It was in drama class, my eighth-grade year. We were studying Shakespeare. During one assignment, my teacher required we memorize the monologue from the play, *Hamlet*.

The infamous speech given by Prince Hamlet that begins with "to be or not to be, that is the question." While I never memorized this monologue, I believe it to be near impossible to forget the opening line. And if I may, I'd like to borrow that quote from Shakespeare's *Hamlet* and tweak the wording, presenting instead, this challenge. To work or not to work, that is the question.

There are no more important questions in life than those questions about where you'll spend eternity and how you'll achieve that timeless destination. Spending forever with Jesus must dominate your life's focus. What is required of me? Do I need to do something? Must I live a certain way to be saved? The question I want to raise to the surface is this: "do I need to do well, for Him to say 'well done'?"

We live in a world where traditions have hijacked and men of influence have manipulated Christian culture. This Gospel is a saving Gospel, and it doesn't need help from tradition. It saves all by itself. We don't need to improve the Gospel. It's His message, and it's the greatest message the world has ever known.

It is my goal in this book to point, not to men of history, but to the Word of God, solely and entirely. So this next question isn't a small question. It could be one of the biggest questions of your life. "What must I do to be saved?" Let's explore this question together.

Jesus

Baptism doesn't matter, they say. Being filled with the Holy Spirit doesn't matter, they say. Living a life that makes God smile it doesn't matter, because those are works and works don't save you.

I have a big problem with that because Jesus had a big problem with that, and if Jesus had a problem with something, then let's make sure that we have a problem with it as well. If Jesus said it's good, then we must also call it good. If Jesus called it sin, we also must call it sin.

I don't think we can overestimate the importance of starting with Jesus. When life presents questions, begin with Jesus in your search for the answers. What did Jesus say? What did Jesus do? What did Jesus think about it?

Salvation comes entirely from Jesus. He's our savior and redeemer. We absolutely must pattern our life after His. We must study what Jesus taught and apply His teachings in our lives. We must discover what mattered to Jesus and make sure those same things matter to us.

If Jesus thought a thing was important, may we never call it unimportant. So, in our quest to answer the question about works, we must start with Jesus. Did Jesus think works were important?

A powerful passage of scripture, found in the Gospels, is the words of Jesus nearing the conclusion of His wondrous sermon on the mount. Jesus talks about the kingdom of heaven. Jesus tells the crowd that not everybody who "says Lord, Lord" can enter heaven, but heaven is for those who "Do the will of my Father." Here is the verse:

Not every one that saith unto me, Lord, Lord, shall enter into the kingdom of heaven; but he that doeth the will of my Father which is in heaven.

Matthew 7:21 (KJV)

Jesus said that it's not enough to just "say," you've got to be willing to "do." "Saying" won't take you to heaven, but "doing" the will of God can. And by definition, "do" is to work, to act, or to execute. In fact, the Greek word translated in KJV English as "Doeth" also means "work."

So, Jesus said heaven's entrance is for "He that DOETH or WORKS the will of my Father" Jesus didn't stop there but He says this in verse 23:

And then will I profess unto them, I never knew you: depart from me, ye that work iniquity.

Matthew 7:23 (KJV)

When Jesus tells the people listening to Him about those who "said Lord, Lord" but weren't ready, Jesus tells them to depart from Him "ye that work iniquity." The reason they were told they weren't accepted into heaven was their works. Modern Christianity says works don't matter, but Jesus said your works have kept you from being saved.

Works are important to Jesus and works matter to Jesus. According to Him, our eternal salvation is inseparably tied to our works.

It's true that works don't save us. God and His grace toward us saves us entirely. And while it is God who does all the saving, we do hold a responsibility to submit to the saving process. It's clear scripturally that our salvation requires our obedience, and that our works do matter.

Jesus made a statement with crystal clarity. He spoke to His disciples and said this:

> *If ye love me, keep my commandments.*
> **John 14:15 (KJV)**

Jesus didn't speak a mystery, but spoke clearly. You cannot profess to love Jesus and not follow His commandments; you cannot love Jesus and not love what He taught; you cannot follow Jesus without following His word; and you cannot believe in Christ without obeying Christ. Your belief in Jesus totally depends on your willingness to obey His word. Paul echoes this sentiment in His letter to Titus, his son, in the faith.

They profess that they know God; but in works they deny him, being abominable, and disobedient, and unto every good work reprobate.

Titus 1:16 (KJV)

They professed to know God, but denied Him in their works. And because of that, Paul labels them abominable and disobedient. That wasn't a new teaching, it was the same thing Jesus had already taught. It's not enough to "say" or "profess" the Lord, but heaven is for them who do the will of God.

It's evident that Jesus cares about what we do in our life. Jesus is quoted five times in three Gospels, saying if anyone desires to follow Him, they must "take up their cross and follow Him." Here is one of the references:

And when he had called the people unto him with his disciples also, he said unto them, Whosoever will come after me, let him deny himself, and take up his cross, and follow me.

Mark 8:34 (KJV)

Jesus didn't tell His followers to believe in Him only, but He told them they must take up their cross. Modern Christian doctrines will tell you to believe in the work of His cross, but Jesus said to carry your cross. Following Jesus is more than simply believing, following Jesus requires someone willing to put in the effort of carrying their cross.

It's not a light thing, it's not a pebble-sized commitment that fits into one's pocket. It's a commitment that is much bigger than yourself. It's a cross that will change your life. It will change how you walk; it will change how you speak; it will change how you think and act. Jesus went even further in another instance,

And whoever does not take his cross and follow me is not worthy of me.

Matthew 10:38 (ESV)

Jesus seems very uncompromising on the issue of carrying the cross. According to Him, it's not enough to believe in His cross, you must carry your own. There's only one with the words to eternal life, and it's not John Calvin, nor Martin Luther. It's Jesus. Build your salvation on His word, and build your life on His commandments. Jesus didn't preach or teach a work-less salvation.

The Apostles

You can learn a lot about a teacher by watching his students. If the students are sincere in following their teacher, then they'll follow the teachings of their teacher. The disciples of Jesus, who would later become apostles, didn't simply "follow" their teacher, they gave their lives for Him.

Jesus's students believed in Him so much they went to their graves proclaiming His message. They faithfully followed until the end. They boldly proclaimed His Gospel, even when they were hated for it. They were arrested and beaten, yet they still preached His message.

Some of them would write the New Testament, and from their powerful teachings, we can learn much more about what was important to Jesus. They were students, writing what they'd learned from their Lord. They weren't writing their own doctrines; they were giving us His doctrines. Let's look at a handful of passages from the students of Christ.

"Salvation is by grace alone, through faith alone." This is the billboard for modern Christianity, and we discussed a few points that showed us that Jesus didn't feel the same way. But we can go even further. We can go to writings of the apostles to discover more and strengthen our belief in Bible salvation.

It comes as no surprise that the Apostles agree with Jesus. In fact, Paul put it so plainly that he tells one church to "work out their own salvation." Here's the reference:

Therefore, my beloved, as you have always obeyed, so now, not only as in my presence but much more in my absence, work out your own salvation with fear and trembling, for it is God who works in you, both to will and to work for his good pleasure.

Philippians 2:12–13 (ESV)

The admonition seems plain. Work out your salvation. Paul follows this statement by saying God is working in you so you may both "will" and "do" of His good pleasure. Let me list a few New Testament scriptures that point directly to the importance of obedience to the Gospel.

He will render to each one <u>according to his works:</u> to those who by patience <u>in well-doing</u> seek for glory and honor and immortality, he will give eternal life; but for those who are self-seeking and <u>do not obey the truth</u>, but obey unrighteousness, there will be wrath and fury.

Romans 2:6–8 (ESV)

And to you who are troubled rest with us, when the Lord Jesus shall be revealed from heaven with his mighty angels, In flaming fire taking vengeance on them that know not God, and that <u>obey not the gospel of our Lord Jesus Christ.</u>

2 Thessalonians 1:7–8 (KJV)

This is a faithful saying, and these things I will that thou affirm constantly, that they which have believed in God might <u>be careful to maintain good works.</u> These things are good and profitable unto men.

Titus 3:8 (KJV)

And being made perfect, he became the author of eternal salvation <u>unto all them that obey him.</u>

Hebrews 5:9 (KJV)

You see that a person is justified by works and not by faith alone.

James 2:24 (ESV)

I must hurry through this topic. This chapter could prove to be very long if I listed every New Testament verse that points to "works" and "obedience."

It's clear biblically; the Apostles preached and taught that your works matter, and that obeying the Gospel matters. Their teaching didn't contradict that of their teacher, Jesus. They run together in perfect harmony. Yes, you must believe in Christ, but you also must follow Christ. You cannot love Jesus and not obey Jesus.

Salvation isn't for the believer, it's for the obedient. Salvation by grace alone, through faith alone, is a gross misinterpretation of scripture that we must correct. We must realign ourselves with the teachings of Christ and His Apostles.

Heads and Tails

It was a hot summer morning in the city of Joplin. My brother and I were doing community outreach on the north side of town. Walking the scorching blacktop roads of a mobile home park, hanging door hangers on doorknobs, and talking to the people we saw outside. It was that morning I met a gentleman outside his home.

I approached him with my normal greeting and conversed with him. It didn't take long for me to realize he was a Calvinist, and was learned in the scriptures. I told him I was a Pentecostal pastor, and it was from there that he began his defense of his faith.

Most of what he said was the normal talking points of a "Grace Alone" salvation. Telling me that works had nothing to do with salvation and that grace was the only thing that saved us. I listened for a moment, then asked him some questions about James chapter 2, (the chapter in which the Apostle James writes explicitly, saying that faith alone cannot save, but it must be paired with works). And his response was new to me. I was a little taken aback for a moment. He responded by saying that the Apostle James didn't have a full revelation of "grace" like the Apostle Paul had.

It was such a bold and dangerous claim that I had to fight to hide the expressions that threatened to show on my face. I replied with the first thought that came to my mind. "That's weird because James was Jesus's brother. You would think that

Jesus told His brother about grace." Looking back, it sounds sarcastic (which wasn't my intention). To give a more leveled response, I would say James was the brother of Christ and pastor of the church in the holy city of Jerusalem. If James didn't know about grace, then something is very amiss.

These are the lengths that the defenders of "work-less" salvation will go, to dismiss entire books of the New Testament because they don't support their faulty doctrines; to accuse the half-brother of Jesus of not having a full understanding of grace, and writing false information to the church.

The truth is the Bible doesn't teach a "work-less" salvation. If you're still with me in this chapter, I'd like to look together at the writings of James to explore the absolutely necessary relationship between faith and works.

James chapter 2 gives us a clear view of the vital connection between our faith and our works. James, so capably and sensitively, writes under the inspiration of the Spirit. James, who is the brother of Jesus, son of Joseph and Mary, pastor of the church in Jerusalem, an apostle of the early church.

His letter is brilliantly written. So much more than the words of James, but the words of God. If you read the second chapter of his letter, you'll find that faith alone doesn't save you. This is a bold statement, considering many Christian denominations have built their entire belief systems on "salvation by faith alone."

I heard one well-known preacher say, "salvation is by faith alone, not faith plus something else." The Bible says otherwise. Let's look at a few verses.

> *What good is it, my brothers, if someone says he has faith but does not have works? Can that faith save him?*
> **James 2:14 (ESV)**

This conversation started with a question. If someone says they have faith but they don't have works, can that faith save him? He doesn't leave us to struggle for the answer, instead he quickly answers,

> *So also faith by itself, if it does not have works, is dead. But someone will say, "You have faith and I have works." Show me your faith apart from your works, and I will show you my faith by my works.*
> **James 2:17–18 (ESV)**

Faith by itself, without works, is dead. James said some say you have faith and I have works, but he ends the verse saying I will show you my faith by my works. Because it's not about having one or the other, but your faith *and* your works (or obedience) must exist together. It's not faith all by itself, it's faith paired with your obedience to the Gospel.

Notice this is exactly what Jesus was saying when He said, "If you love me, keep my commandments." It's not love all by itself, it's love plus obedience. James isn't writing a new message; he's continuing the message Jesus preached.

By this point in the conversation, James has made a significant point, however he doesn't end there. He continues to hammer the same nail to solidify the point.

> *Do you want to be shown, you foolish person, that faith apart from works is useless? Was not Abraham our father justified by works when he offered up his son Isaac on the altar? You see that faith was active along with his works, and faith was completed by his works.*
>
> **James 2:20–22 (ESV)**

James says it is a foolish person who doesn't believe works matter. It's foolish to deny that obeying the directives of scripture is important to your salvation. James pulls from the Old Testament to further bolster this message, giving a brief shout out to Abraham and then finishing by saying that "faith was active along with his works, and faith was completed by his works."

Once again, James has made a very clear and elaborate statement on the issue, but he still feels to take it one step further, and he even reaches back to yet another Old Testament character to provide more clarity,

> *You see that a person is justified by works and not by faith alone. And in the same way was not also Rahab the prostitute justified by works when she received the messengers and sent them out by another way? For as the body apart from the spirit is dead, so also faith apart from works is dead.*
>
> **James 2:24–26 (ESV)**

This time it's Rahab who gets the honorable mention, and James uses her story in the same way he used Abraham's. To prove that faith alone is dead. It's work plus faith, faith plus work. Not one or the other, but both working in tandem. They're not two different coins, but two sides of the same coin. Heads and tails. Faith in the Gospel of Jesus, and obeying the Gospel of Jesus.

The well-known preacher I spoke of earlier said, "Salvation is by faith alone, not faith plus something else." The Bible says it's faith plus works.

The Christian author A.W. Tozer is quoted as saying this:

The Bible recognizes no faith that does not lead to obedience, nor does it recognize any obedience that does not spring from faith. The two are at opposite sides of the same coin.

—A. W. Tozer

Faith and works, heads and tails. Two sides of one coin. Either of those components by themselves don't save you, but bringing them together can. Believing in His cross and obeying His commands.

This chapter is already heavy on information, and there's so much more I want to write about regarding this topic. But for the sake of brevity, let me give a few final scriptural examples of belief and works being paired together to bring about salvation.

But when <u>they believed</u> Philip preaching the things concerning the kingdom of God, and the name of Jesus Christ, <u>they were baptized</u>, both men and women.

Acts 8:12 (KJV)

And as they went on their way, they came unto a certain water: and the eunuch said, See, here is water; what doth hinder me *to be baptized? And Philip said, If thou believest with all thine heart, thou mayest. And he answered and said, <u>I believe that Jesus Christ is the Son of God</u>. And he commanded the chariot to stand still: and they went down both into the water, both Philip and the eunuch; <u>and he baptized him</u>.*

Acts 8:36–38 (KJV)

He said unto them, <u>Have ye received the Holy Ghost since ye believed?</u> And they said unto him, We have not so much as heard whether there be any Holy Ghost.

Acts 19:2 (KJV)

This is what the writer of James was saying: its faith in Christ paired with your obedience to Christ. Heads and tails.

The Church of Acts

We find perhaps one of the most famous scriptures in the church in the book of Acts. This time, it was the Apostle Peter who spoke. Peter is nearing the end of his very first sermon. He's preaching the Gospel of Christ to a crowd of people in the streets of Jerusalem. Following Peter's sermon, a man in the crowd presents the question on every heart, "What must we do?" And Peter speaks in response to this question, saying this,

Then Peter said unto them, Repent, and be baptized every one of you in the name of Jesus Christ for the remission of sins, and ye shall receive the gift of the Holy Ghost.

Acts 2:38 (KJV)

That is the proper response to the Gospel. According to Peter, you must repent, be baptized in the name of Jesus, and receive the Holy Ghost. Notice that Peter wasn't preaching a new message, but was the student repeating the teacher.

- Jesus preached repentance (Matthew 4:17)
- Jesus said that a man must be born of water and of Spirit (John 3:5)
- Jesus said a man must believe and be baptized to be saved (Mark 16:16)
- Jesus commanded His disciples to go teach and baptize all people from all nations (Matthew 28:19)
- Jesus told them they would receive power after the Holy Ghost comes upon them (Acts 1:8)

Peter was a student, echoing the words of his teacher. He didn't preach a new message, but he preached the same thing Jesus did. Repentance, water baptism, and being filled with the Holy Ghost. Peter did more than preach water baptism. He also commanded this in Acts, chapter 10.

And he commanded them to be baptized in the name of the Lord. Then prayed they him to tarry certain days.

Acts 10:48 (KJV)

Water baptism is more than a New Testament teaching, it's a New Testament command. The point I'm trying to present is this: our response to the Gospel matters. It's more than just hearing the Gospel and believing the Gospel. We must also obey the Gospel.

There's a biblical response to His message of salvation. It is repenting your sins, having your sins washed away in water baptism, and receiving the Spirit of God. What you do matters. Your obedience matters.

Salvation apart from obedience is unknown in the sacred Scriptures… Apart from obedience there can be no salvation, for salvation without obedience is a self-contradictory impossibility.

—A. W. Tozer

To escape the error of salvation by works we have fallen into the opposite error of salvation without obedience. In our eagerness to get rid of the legalistic doctrine of works we have thrown out the baby with the bath and gotten rid of obedience as well.

—A. W. Tozer

8
Letters to the Bride

He brought me to the banqueting house, and his banner over me was love.

—Solomon

In the beginning God created the heavens and the earth. The earth was without form, and void; darkness was on the face of the deep. And the Spirit of God moved upon the face of the waters. The opening scene of holy scripture takes us into the chaotic and formless beginning of His work. All was void; darkness covered the canvas. There was no form; there was no structure.

From our vantage point, there'd seem to be no potential in this swirling, topsy-turvy, disarrayed darkness. However, God knows how to bring peace into the pandemonium. God knows how to command chaos to calm.

In the middle of that undeveloped planet, God's Spirit moved over the water. In a way only God can, He established order. He started with light. With a few words from His mouth, light burst onto to the scene.

Everything that was hidden by the dark before was revealed. All the potential that was hiding in the shadows was visible. From there, God creates. He brings dry land out of the water; separating continents from oceans and mountains from prairies.

From the dirt, life buds. Towering trees, blooming flowers, and delicious fruit rise from the soil. Animals of all kinds: the mammals on land, fish for the sea, and birds in the sky.

God ends His work of creation with His ultimate piece. It appears every move He made up until that point was for a last move. Everything created before that moment was, in fact, for this moment. When God reached into the dirt and formed a human body. God breathed into that body the breath of life and man became a living soul.

All of creation pointed to that one act. Each day of creation ended with a finger lifted towards this event. God made everything man needed for survival first, then made man. Earth wasn't created for God; God created earth for man.

So much so that after man inhaled his first breath of oxygen, God addressed him, saying, "I have given you every plant yielding seed, and every beast of the earth and every bird of the sky. And everything that has in it, the breath of life. I have given it to you."

And in His own image, God created Adam and gave him life. And like a gift carefully wrapped for a loved one, God handed the earth over to the hands of man. You see, God didn't create the earth for Himself; God created it for man.

God's desire was and is a relationship. He wanted someone He could love, and someone who would freely love Him in return. God wasn't after the trees and birds; God was after man. God calmed the chaos and built a home for the people He'd give all His love, too. God turned the lights of the universe on, not so He could see, but so we could see. All of this was for us, and all of us were for Him. God created earth for man, but God created man for Him.

I believe it's vital that we understand who we are to God. To see ourselves the way God sees us will open new doors of purpose in our lives. To understand we're more than created creatures; God formed you and fashioned you with a very specific purpose.

God didn't create us to be a part of nature's food chain or ecosystem. God created you and me to be in a relationship with Him. We are called to love God and be loved by God. We are called to be His bride.

The Bride of Christ

It was God's desire to love and be loved that drove Him to reach into the dirt of the earth and create man. God created us because He wanted a bride. In multiple scripture passages, God's people or God's church, is referred to as a bride. In fact, when we all get to heaven, the Bible tells us we will take part in the "marriage supper of the Lamb." Here's the scripture reference:

Let us rejoice and exult and give him the glory, for the marriage of the Lamb has come, and his Bride has made herself ready; it was granted her to clothe herself with fine linen, bright and pure—for the fine linen is the righteous deeds of the saints. And the angel said to me, "Write this: Blessed are those who are invited to the marriage supper of the Lamb." And he said to me, "These are the true words of God."

Revelation 19:7–9 (ESV)

Heaven is for Jesus and His bride, the church. What a beautiful picture of how God looks at His people. He loves us. We are called the apple of His eye, and the Bible says God is mindful of us. What a powerful truth we can hold. God doesn't think about us occasionally; God's mind is full of us.

The church is more than a gathering of people; the church is the bride of Christ, and we are being prepared for a marriage in heaven. God's original desire was to have a companion; a people made in His image. People that would carry His name, the same way a bride carries the name of her husband.

However, sin created a barrier that separated God from those He loved. From there, the rest of the Bible tells the story of God tearing down the barriers that separated Him from His bride.

I've written so much in this chapter only to delete it for the sake of time and staying on topic. I could say so much about the love of God. However, the point I want to make for this chapter is this: the people of God are the bride. The church is the bride. Not the world, but the church.

The church isn't an optional gathering you can choose to be a part of or not. Your relationship with and your involvement in the church is directly tied to your salvation. After all, God isn't coming back to take *you* home. He's coming to take the *bride* home.

Some say church isn't important. They say going to church doesn't matter in the scope of salvation. I strongly and loudly disagree! Everything God has done from the beginning until now was ultimately for the church.

The reason Jesus died on the cross was for the church. Scripture tells us Jesus purchased the church with His own blood.

We mistakenly think when God comes back, He's coming back for us individually, but the Bible tells us God is coming back for His church. He isn't coming for you; He's coming for the church. The question is, are you a part of the church?

Jesus isn't marrying many brides; He's marrying *the* bride. If you want to be a part of that marriage in heaven, you need to be a part of the bride. With that said, going to church is vitally important because we're coming together as one body, one church, or one bride.

I had one person tell me, "I love God, but I don't love church." That's impossible. How can you love God but not love His body? There's only one train that's going to heaven, and that's the church. Get your ticket and get on the train.

I apologize for getting off topic, but I fear that too many undervalue their relationship with the church. The point I want to make with this section is: the church is the bride, not the world. The bride is those who have come into the church, been born again, and have begun their relationship with God. With this knowledge, we learn a principle that will help us understand and interpret New Testament scriptures.

Not Your Mail

Modern day Christianity has consistently made the mistake of misinterpreting scriptures in the New Testament. Particularly in what we call the Epistles or letters. In their misguided interpretation, they've complicated the simplicity found in Christ. Specifically, regarding the topic of salvation.

Taking verses from the Epistles or letters; verses that seem to say what they're looking for and building their doctrines off them. If you take Romans chapter 10, isolate it, and read it with no context, and you don't harmonize it with the rest of the scriptures, then you can easily tell people they don't need to be baptized.

Even though Jesus said to be baptized, Paul said in Romans 10 that all you need to do is believe. These flawed attempts at interpreting scripture have caused millions of Christians to be misled, misguided, and, in some cases, lost.

The most important question in life is, how can I be saved? What is required of me to go to heaven? It's something we must never be confused about. We cannot hope to stumble into salvation, we must make our utmost and best efforts to be saved. We mustn't allow a misguided Christianity to confuse us.

So, how do we interpret these passages of scripture? Verses that say we only need to call on the name of the Lord to be saved? Or confess with your mouth and believe in your heart and you shall be saved? Let me give Romans 10 as an example:

Because, if you confess with your mouth that Jesus is Lord and believe in your heart that God raised him from the dead, you will

be saved. For with the heart one believes and is justified, and with the mouth one confesses and is saved.
Romans 10:9–10 (ESV)

For "everyone who calls on the name of the Lord will be saved."
Romans 10:13 (ESV)

These verses can be very confusing for some. Why does Romans 10 contradict the book of Acts, and the many teachings of Jesus? Are the scriptures not in agreement? Which one should I follow? I want to present a Bible study principle that will help tremendously when reading the New Testament, and more specifically, in what we call the Epistles.

The principle is this: all of Paul's Epistles are "letters to the bride." He wrote them unanimously to people who have already become a part of the church or the bride. Paul was writing to churches that already experienced the first steps of becoming born again.

For example, Paul wrote the book of Romans to an already established church in the great city of ancient wonder, the city of Rome. We read this in the very first chapter of the book,

<u>To all that be in Rome, beloved of God, called to be saints</u>: Grace to you and peace from God our Father, and the Lord Jesus Christ. First, I thank my God through Jesus Christ for you all, <u>that your faith is spoken of throughout the whole world.</u>
Romans 1:7–8 (KJV)

Paul acknowledges, at the very beginning of his letter, that he's writing to the saints of the church in Rome. He goes so far to say, "your faith is spoken of throughout the whole word." These people aren't new converts; they've been around long enough to have a reputation for having great faith.

A reputation not limited to their own circle, but word had spread throughout the land, that the people in the church of Rome are faithful people.

It's so important that we understand the people Paul is writing to have already been baptized. This isn't my speculation, but once again, Paul acknowledged it in the letter.

Know ye not, that <u>so many of us as were baptized</u> into Jesus Christ were baptized into his death? <u>Therefore we are buried with him by baptism</u> into death: that like as Christ was raised up from the dead by the glory of the Father, even so we also should walk in newness of life. For if <u>we have been</u> planted together in the likeness of his death, we shall be also in the likeness of his resurrection:

Romans 6:3–5 (KJV)

Four chapters prior to Romans chapter 10, Paul addresses the fact that he was writing to "baptized" people. Paul says, "so many of US as were baptized," and also "Therefore WE are buried with him by baptism." It's clear that the people Paul is writing to are believers who have already taken the first steps of salvation.

So, when Paul writes in Romans chapter 10 that we only need to confess and believe to be saved, he's writing to already established believers. He isn't giving them instructions on how to begin their salvation, rather, he's telling them how to continue in their salvation.

Paul's letters are all written to people who are already part of the bride. For the sake of time, I'll only expound on Romans 10, but to help solidify this point, let me give a few more examples of Paul identifying his audience in his letters.

<u>Unto the church of God</u> which is at Corinth, <u>to them that are sanctified</u> in Christ Jesus, called to be saints, with all that in every place call upon the name of Jesus Christ our Lord, both theirs and ours:
1 Corinthians 1:2 (KJV)

Paul, an apostle of Jesus Christ by the will of God, to the saints which are at Ephesus, and to the faithful in Christ Jesus:
Ephesians 1:1 (KJV)

Paul and Timotheus, the servants of Jesus Christ, <u>to all the saints in Christ Jesus which are at Philippi</u>, with the bishops and deacons:
Philippians 1:1 (KJV)

<u>To the saints and faithful brethren in Christ</u> which are at Colosse: Grace be unto you, and peace, from God our Father and the Lord Jesus Christ.
Colossians 1:2 (KJV)

You'll see this greeting in all of Paul's letters directed to churches. Paul's writings are letters written specifically to established churches. They're letters to the bride. They're letters written to men and women who have already begun their walk with God. Paul isn't explaining how to begin salvation, he's explaining how to continue your salvation.

They're letters for people who have already been born again, as Jesus and the apostles commanded them to be. So, I'd contend that there are entire books of the Bible that don't apply to you until you've been born again. If you aren't part of "the bride," then the letters aren't for you yet. You're reading someone else's mail.

How then should we interpret Romans 10? We must interpret it in a way that harmonizes with the rest of scripture. Paul isn't saying that baptism isn't necessary to be saved. After all, Paul has already established, four chapters prior, that they have been baptized into Christ.

However, Paul is reminding these men and women that they still have a responsibility to continue believing and confessing the word of faith, and confessing that Jesus Christ is Lord.

Just because you've obeyed the first steps of the Gospel doesn't mean you can sit down and do nothing. Just because you've been baptized doesn't mean you can put on cruise control, sit back, and enjoy the ride. If you continue to read the chapter, Paul explains why it's important they continue believing and confessing.

For there is no distinction between Jew and Greek; for the same Lord is Lord of all, bestowing his riches on all who call on him. For "everyone who calls on the name of the Lord will be saved." How then will they call on him in whom they have not believed? And how are they to believe in him of whom they have never heard? And how are they to hear without someone preaching? And how are they to preach unless they are sent? As it is written, "How beautiful are the feet of those who preach the good news!"

Romans 10:12–15 (ESV)

Paul is telling the church in Rome two things. First, Paul is telling them that whoever calls on the name of the Lord shall be saved. In other words, anybody can take part in this great salvation. It isn't limited to a certain skin tone or language group, but absolutely anybody willing to call on the name of the Lord can be saved.

The second thing that Paul is telling them is that while anybody can call on the name of the Lord, not everybody knows how to call on the name of the Lord; not everyone knows what it means to call on the name of the Lord.

How can they call on something they don't believe in? How can they believe in a message they haven't heard? And how will they ever hear this great message unless someone preaches it to them?

Paul is telling them to preach the Gospel. To tell the people of Rome what it means to call on the name of the Lord. Tell everybody that Jesus can save and Jesus can deliver. Paul tops it all off by saying this:

So faith comes from hearing, and hearing through the word of Christ.

Romans 10:17 (ESV)

This is why it's so important that we confess with our mouth that Jesus is Lord. It builds faith; it saves the sinner; it delivers the addicted; and it pushes back darkness.

Paul isn't saying to believe and confess one time and you will be saved. Paul is saying it doesn't matter how long you've been in the church, keep confessing Jesus. It doesn't matter if you've been in the church all your life; keep confessing Jesus.

Don't discount any man or woman because of who they are, where they come from, or what their disposition in life is. Everybody has access to the name. Everybody is invited to call on the name of the Lord for salvation. Now go tell everyone you can tell.

They cannot know Jesus unless you show Jesus. So go, preach Jesus; teach Jesus; live Jesus; talk Jesus. This saving message is the greatest thing on the face of this planet, and everybody deserves to know about the one who died for their sins.

We are called to be the Bride of Christ. The bride takes on the name of the groom and the bride carries the name of the groom. So again, I say, they cannot know Jesus unless you show Jesus.

Conclusion

So, I end this chapter with this. Paul wrote the Epistles to the bride/church. He wrote them to people who already took the first steps of New Testament salvation. They're not instructions on how to begin your salvation; they're instructions on how to continue your salvation.

We begin our salvation with repentance, water baptism, and being filled with the Spirit. This is clear through the teachings of Christ in the Gospels and throughout the teaching of the Acts of the Apostles.

If you're on a quest to be saved, start with Jesus. Once you've been adopted into this wonderful and unparalleled family of God, then so much more will be opened for you. There are storehouses of revelation that are available to the Bride of Christ. Are you part of "the bride"?

9
A New Name

What is his name, and what is his son's name?

—Solomon

God called a people for a purpose. The call of God always comes with purpose. God is a God of purpose. Every move He makes is for a reason. There are no accidents with God. There are no mess ups with God. If God called you, He did so on purpose and for a purpose. Regardless of whether you deserve it, regardless of whether you can carry out the calling. Because God doesn't call the worthy, and God doesn't call the ones who deserve goodness. There are none who are worthy of the call before the call.

There are none that rightfully deserve His goodness. We're recipients of beautiful grace and loving mercy. He calls the unworthy and makes them worthy. He calls the insignificant and makes them significant. God gracefully welcomes us into His glorious plan of redemption. Even though we don't deserve it, He calls for us. He reaches for us. He wants us.

The Apostle John powerfully penned these words, "while we were yet sinners, Christ died for us." Jesus loved us when we were unlovable. Jesus loved you when you didn't love yourself.

He pursued you while you turned your back to Him. He's always had a plan for your life. There has never been a moment where God gave up on you. Through all the mangled messes in your past, through all the shame and regret of your story, God has always had a plan. While you were chasing your own dreams of success and happiness, God has waited patiently in line. He's been waiting for the moment you'd turn to Him and hear His call.

God is always calling. The question is, are we always listening? Never let yourself believe the lie that God cannot use or call you. You haven't fallen so low that God can't reach down and pick you up. You haven't outrun God's purpose. Your sin hasn't disqualified you, because where sin abounds, His grace doth abound more. You're not too broken, you're not too far gone, and you're not too insignificant.

With each rising of the sun, God's mercies are new. God has a plan for you. God has a purpose for you. Your past will never catch up to God's future for your life. He loves you; not because you're good, but because He's good. It doesn't matter what your name is. God wants to give you a new name. God's purpose is a new name. God's calling is to receive and carry a new name.

I want to show you in the scripture that it doesn't matter who you are and what your name is, God is calling you. God isn't calling you for your name, He's calling you for His name. His purpose is a new name. What if I told you your salvation depended on you receiving a new name? Let's go to scripture.

We are told in the Bible that God's purpose for calling out a nation was for His name.

Simeon hath declared how God at the first did visit the Gentiles, to take out of them a people for his name.

Acts 15:14 (KJV)

God called a people for a very specific purpose; to carry His name. We see this from the very beginning, when the population of the earth restarted with Noah's family. Noah had three sons: Shem, Ham, and Japheth.

Of these three lineages, God chose one to be His people. God chose Shem's lineage. It's interesting to note that "Shem" means "Name." The people that God chose are the people of Shem or the people of the name. From those people, He called a man named Abram. God called Abram out of his father's country, telling him, "If you will go where I tell you to go, I will make of you a great nation. If you will do what I ask of you, I will bless you and your family Abram. Look up Abram, try to count the shimmering stars of the night sky. Just as you cannot count the number of stars, neither shall you be able to count the number of your children."

God makes a new covenant with the man named Abram. When He makes the covenant with Abram, God changes his name to Abraham. Not only does God give a new covenant, but with this new covenant, God gives a new name. Not only to Abram but to Abram's wife, Sarai. Abram would be called Abraham, and Sarai would be called Sarah.

That is the first family of the new covenant. It's the very beginning of God's people, and God said His people would begin with a new name. Remember, God wants a people to carry His name, not another name. So, from the very start, God established a principle. God's people wouldn't be built on their own name, but on a new name that God gave them. It isn't limited to Abraham, nor does it stop with Sarah, but God continues that principle with their grandchildren.

God chose Jacob, the grandson of Abraham and Sarah, to be the continuation of God's nation. More than just the continuation, it was also from Jacob that God named His people. God chose Jacob to be the namesake. Once again, God didn't use the name given by the parents. Instead, God gave Jacob a new name.

On the top of a mount, Jacob wrestled with an angel of the Lord, desperately trying to hold on. When the angel asked Jacob to let him go, Jacob said, "I will not let you go until you bless me." There are many sermons and powerful points we can draw from this scene of scripture, however, I must hasten to my point. The Lord relents; He blesses Jacob and gives him a new name.

And he said, Thy name shall be called no more Jacob, but Israel: for as a prince hast thou power with God and with men, and hast prevailed.

Genesis 32:28 (KJV)

Notice that Jacob asks for a blessing and God gives him a new name. There's no greater thing you can receive from God than a new name and a new identity. God blesses Jacob with a new name saying, "your name will now be Israel."

And from then on, God's people were called Israel. Even today, in 2023, the nation of Israel stands alive and strong. Not the nation of Jacob, or the people of Jacob, but the nation of Jacob's new name. God showed the world that His kingdom would begin with a new name, a name that would come from God, not from man.

It's always been God's desire to have a people who carries His name. Don't believe me? Here's a scripture reference:

And the Gentiles shall see thy righteousness, and all kings thy glory: and <u>thou shalt be called by a new name</u>, <u>which the mouth of the LORD shall name.</u>

Isaiah 62:2 (KJV)

God's desire was for a people who would be called a new name, which the mouth of the Lord shall name. The new name comes from God, not from man. This powerful truth isn't limited to the Old Testament. In fact, it's in the New Testament where this essential truth comes to complete fruition. Let's continue our journey together; and let God be true.

The Name Revealed

Earlier in the book, we spoke briefly of John the Baptist. The cousin of Jesus, born only a few months earlier. John was a powerful preacher. He was called to be the forerunner of Christ, meaning John came before Christ and his ministry acted as an introduction to Jesus. He was specifically called to "prepare the way of the Lord."

John's ministry prepared the way for Jesus. He paved the road Jesus walked. John preached promises that Jesus himself would later fulfill. More so, John prepared the way of the Lord before John ever preached a sermon or baptized a sinner for repentance. John prepared the way of the Lord from the moment he received life in the womb of his mother, Elisabeth.

First, John prepared the way of the Lord because his conception was a miraculous conception, as John's mother was barren her entire life. She received a healing from God for the sole purpose of having this son, not to mention Elisabeth was over eighty years old when she received God's promise and bore her child. This miraculous conception within the womb of a barren, eighty-year-old woman was a foreshadowing of the miraculous conception of Jesus in the womb of the virgin girl, Mary. John was conceived miraculously. Then, a few months later, Jesus was also conceived miraculously; because John prepared the way of the Lord.

There is more on John's miraculous birth later in chapter 11, "Born to Live," but for now, let's focus on a different point. The name John received. This parallel is much deeper than just the miracle of a baby in the womb, but the names both children received were a powerful continuation of what God had started in the very beginning with Abraham.

God began His covenant with Abraham by giving him a new name, a name God chose for him. Then Jacob received the name of Israel, a name chosen not by Jacob, but by God Himself. Because God's kingdom will be built on the name He gives.

The same is true with the baby in Elisabeth's womb, the one who would prepare the way for Christ. When the angel announced the good news of healing to Elisabeth's husband—Zachariah—the angel actually tells them what to name the child.

But the angel said unto him, Fear not, Zacharias: for thy prayer is heard; and thy wife Elisabeth shall bear thee a son, and thou shalt call his name John.
Luke 1:13 (KJV)

So, God not only gives them the promise of a child, but God gives them the name. Zachariah didn't believe the word from the angel. After all, he was a very old man and his wife had never been able to have children. Because of his unbelief, Zachariah is unable to speak until the baby is born. The word of the Lord comes true, and Elisabeth is with child, but Zachariah's ability to talk has been taken away for the duration of the pregnancy. When the baby is born, since his father cannot talk, the people name the child Zachariah after his father, but Elisabeth speaks up and says no, his name will be John. That confused the people because nobody in their family was named John.

And on the eighth day they came to circumcise the child. And they would have called him Zechariah after his father, but his mother answered, "No; he shall be called John." And they said to her, "None of your relatives is called by this name."
Luke 1:59–61 (ESV)

It didn't make sense that they'd give the boy a name that had absolutely nothing to do with their family or history, but it wasn't about their family or their history, it was about God's family and God's future.

They asked Zachariah for clarification. Surely Zachariah wanted his son named after him. Zachariah still can't talk, so he takes a writing tablet and writes "His name is John" and they are in wonder at that. Why would they choose a new name that had nothing to do with their family? The people didn't understand what Zachariah and Elisabeth understood. That child was the beginning of a new work God was doing on earth, and God always begins His work with a new name He gives.

And he asked for a writing tablet and wrote, "His name is John." And they all wondered. And immediately his mouth was opened and his tongue loosed, and he spoke, blessing God.
Luke 1:63–64 (ESV)

That child, the child that prepared "the way of the Lord" began life with a new name. Giving us a glimpse that "the way of the Lord" would begin with a new name.

It's also very interesting to note that when Zachariah wrote "his name would be John," his tongue was immediately loosed. When you get the name right, your tongue will be loosed. But that's not for this chapter. Maybe we can talk about that in chapter 10 "The Gift"

Here's the powerful principle that echoes through the entirety of scripture; God's people will have a new name. That culminates in the birth of Jesus Christ. When the angel Gabriel shows up to speak to Mary and tells her she will be with child, Gabriel gives her explicit instructions. "You shall call his name Jesus."

And the angel said to her, "Do not be afraid, Mary, for you have found favor with God. And behold, you will conceive in your womb and bear a son, and you shall call his name Jesus."

Luke 1:30–31 (ESV)

The Messiah; the Christ; the savior of the world would be named Jesus. Mary, the child you will carry, will be from the Holy Ghost. He will be no ordinary child, but the son of God. Everything your people have been waiting for will be found in Him. You will find salvation in Him. We will find redemption in Him. Deliverance found in Him.

Here is your responsibility. Name Him Jesus. Mary, you don't get to name your first child. God will. The kingdom won't be built on a name that comes from man or woman; it will be built on the name that comes from God. John and Jesus had so much in common. It is wonderful to look at all the parallels in their lives. Both had a supernatural birth, both preached repentance and baptism, both spent time in the wilderness, the Romans arrested and executed both, and for the sake of this chapter, God named them both. Because God began His kingdom with a new name; a name He gives.

So, with that being said, we too must receive a new name. If we want to be a part of God's work on this earth, we must take the name of our savior. Today, under this glorious new covenant, we're called to take on a new name. It's not a name we receive from man or woman; it's God's name. We're called to take on the name of God. The truth is this; I need a new name; I need His name. The question is, how do we take on Jesus's name? This question is of utmost importance, and it takes us into the next section of the chapter.

Water Baptism

Can I begin this subsection with a direct answer to the previous question? We take on Jesus's name through water baptism. We've looked at baptism under multiple lights, through a variety of lenses, and from a few angles.

Together, we've walked through the stories of the Old Testament to discover the truths about baptism. We've also looked at it from John the baptizers unorthodox, yet powerful preaching. I would like to address it directly at this time, from the perspective of New Testament scripture.

It's intriguing to know just how much scripture in the New Testament speaks of baptism. Baptism, without a doubt, is a core teaching in the first century church, with many of the early apostles teaching it. Let me clarify, I don't believe that baptism is what saves you; God saves you. Scripturally speaking, it's definitely an essential part of the process.

I believe that sincere repentance is necessary, and most of Christendom would agree with that statement, however those same people that say repentance is necessary will say that water baptism is unnecessary. Fortunately, the Bible has given us a very good number of scriptures that read clearly.

In previous chapters, we've talked about both John the Baptist and Jesus; they both thought baptism was vitally important. Jesus even dedicated His last words to His disciples, commanding them to go teach and baptize others. You can reference the previous chapters for their words on the subject. I'll focus on the Book of Acts and the New Testament Epistles.

The birth of the church happens in Acts chapter 2. A prayer meeting in an upper room, a unity of mind and purpose. A mighty rushing wind, spiritual fire settling onto the heads of the men and women gathered there. They spoke in tongues as God filled them with His Spirit. When their revival experience spilled onto the streets of Jerusalem, the people of the city were astounded. Some mocked that happening, which prompted Simon Peter to preach the Gospel to those in the streets of Jerusalem. At the end of his first Gospel message, the people in the crowd were touched in their heart and they asked, "What shall we do?" Peter responded with this:

Then Peter said unto them, Repent, and be baptized every one of you in the name of Jesus Christ for the remission of sins, and ye shall receive the gift of the Holy Ghost.

Acts 2:38 (KJV)

It's the sermon that launches God's revival into the streets of Jerusalem, which was the beginning of a worldwide revival that continues even today. Peter's first sermon was monumental. Peter didn't standalone, but he stood with the other eleven apostles and preached the Gospel of the Lord.

The people listening that day were touched by what they heard and felt. They questioned Peter about what they needed to do, and he answered clearly and powerfully, "you must repent and be baptized every one of you in the name of Jesus Christ for the remission of sins and receive the gift of the Holy Ghost." That was the God-given and God-established response to the Gospel.

That first sermon by Peter wasn't the last time it was preached on in the book of Acts. In fact, it was a very common theme in the book of Acts. In Acts chapter 10, Peter commanded them to be baptized,

> *Can any man forbid water, that these should not be baptized, which have received the Holy Ghost as well as we? And <u>he commanded them to be baptized in the name of the Lord.</u> Then prayed they him to tarry certain days.*
>
> ### Acts 10:47–48 (KJV)

The book of Acts is full of baptism. One cannot read the book of Acts with an open mind and not conclude that water baptism was foundational for the church. It's not limited to Acts chapters 2 and 10, it's also in chapters 2, 8, 9, 10, 16, 18, 19, and 22. Baptism wasn't a side note for the apostles. Baptism was central. Baptism was foundational. Baptism was inseparable from salvation.

It was the Apostle Paul who encountered a group of disciples who followed John the Baptist. In Acts 19, we receive a welcoming place to listen in on the conversation that took place. Allow me to paraphrase this encounter. After I paraphrase, I'll put the passage below. Paul speaks to John's disciples, giving them a very direct question: "Have you received the Holy Ghost since you believed?" The disciples of John replied with a confused yet anticipant response, "We haven't heard whether there be any Holy Ghost?"

In this dialogue, we see the utmost importance to this water and Spirit paradigm. Paul didn't open the conversation with doctrinal questions, but begins with questions about their personal experience with God. His very first question was this: have you received the Spirit of God?

Paul, assuming they're disciples and they believe in Christ, that they've already been water baptized. On that assumption, he jumps straight to the infilling of the Holy Ghost. Have you received the Holy Ghost? When he receives their response, and knows their understanding of the Gospel is more limited, he doesn't double down on the Holy Ghost. He doesn't launch into a Bible study on the infilling of the Spirit. Instead, he puts the Holy Ghost question on the shelf and says this, "unto what then were you baptized?"

Their limited understanding of the Spirit prompted Paul to take a few steps back and ask about water baptism. Well, if you haven't heard of the Holy Ghost, then how were you baptized? The word "then" in Paul's response directly points to the information he just received. If you don't have the Spirit, *then* what about the water?

The disciples of John tell him they've been baptized, but it was through John's baptism. You would think Paul would take that new information, rejoice that the disciples had been water baptized, and reach back to the shelf to grab the Holy Ghost question, but he doesn't. Instead, Paul pinpoints his focus on water baptism. Paul tells the disciples, "John baptized unto repentance, telling the people to believe in the one who was to come after him, that is Jesus Christ." Paul was telling them that the baptism of John wasn't sufficient, they had to be baptized unto Jesus's baptism. When they heard that, they were baptized again in the name of Jesus, and then after the water baptism, the Holy Ghost filled them.

It's so powerful to note that after realizing their lack of understanding, he put the Holy Ghost question to the side, and instead anchored his efforts on the fact that they must be baptized unto Jesus's baptism. Once their understanding of baptism was brought up to speed and they were re-baptized in the name of Jesus Christ, the disciples received the Holy Ghost.

It's abundantly evident, Paul believed that water baptism was *just* as important as Spirit baptism. Remember, they followed the teachings of their savior. Jesus said, "Unless a man is born of water and of Spirit, he can't enter the kingdom of God." Paul's focus was identical to Jesus's focus. Have you received the Spirit? No? Then what about the water? Here's the scripture passage:

> *He said unto them, Have ye received the Holy Ghost since ye believed? And they said unto him, We have not so much as heard whether there be any Holy Ghost. And he said unto them, Unto what then were ye baptized? And they said, Unto John's baptism. Then said Paul, John verily baptized with the baptism of repentance, saying unto the people, that they should believe on him which should come after him, that is, on Christ Jesus. When they heard this, they were baptized in the name of the Lord Jesus.*
> **Acts 19:2–5 (KJV)**

One may ask why water baptism was so important? Some have said, "It seems silly to make someone go take a bath to be saved." The first answer is this: it's God's kingdom, and He gets to make the rules. The fact is, God could've chosen anything He wanted to choose to be His instrument of salvation, but He chose water. I've even heard it said that water baptism is only symbolic. However, the scripture tells us it's more than symbolic. According to scripture, water baptism washes away our sins,

> *And now why tarriest thou? arise, and be baptized, and wash away thy sins, calling on the name of the Lord.*
>
> **Acts 22:16 (KJV)**

Acts 2:38 tells us that baptism is "for the remission of our sins." It's more than just symbolic, it has a purpose. In fact, all three initial components of salvation have a significant purpose. Repentance covers your sins with the blood of Christ; baptism washes those sins away, and when you are filled with the Holy Ghost, you receive power to live a life victorious over sin. To reject water baptism is to reject part of biblical salvation.

Let me make this clarification: it's not the water that saves you, and it's not the water that washes away your sins; it's God who does those things. The water is the point of obedience.

We can look back at a man in the Old Testament. His name was Naaman. He had tragically contracted the skin disease known as leprosy, and when he heard that the God of Israel could heal him, he traveled to meet with the prophet Elisha. The man of God instructed Naaman to dip in the river of Jordan seven times, and though Naaman was upset with that response, he eventually went to the river and dipped seven times. When he exited the water the seventh time, his skin was completely healed. The water of the Jordan river did *not* have any healing properties. It wasn't the water of the Jordan that took away his leprosy; it was God. The water was the point of obedience. God said to dip in the Jordan and when he obeyed, he was healed.

Even though it was God who healed him and not the water, there wouldn't have been healing without the water. It's the same today; it's God who takes your sins away, not the water. However, without the water, your sins won't be taken away.

Even after the wonderful and power filled chapters of the book of Acts, baptism is taught through the Epistles of Paul and Peter (Romans 6; 1 Corinthians 1, 6, 10, and 12; Galatians 3; Ephesians 4; Colossians 2; Hebrews 6; and 1 Peter 3) further solidifying how important water baptism was to the Apostles of our Lord Jesus Christ. To them, it was a core teaching, and to them, it was an essential part of the Gospel picture.

Baptism was even tied to Jesus on the cross of Calvary. As Paul says, "we are buried with Him in baptism." To refuse water baptism is to refuse the Gospel of Christ.

To circle back to the point I made at the beginning of this section, baptism is how we take on the name of Jesus Christ. We're called to take on a new name, more specifically we're called to take on His name. There's only one name that can save you. It's the name of Jesus. No matter how great your name is, it will never be great enough to save you from sin.

Jesus is the only name that can cleanse the stains of sin in your life. Take His name. Submit to His name. Put on His name. Scripture admonishes us to "Put on Christ."

But put ye on the Lord Jesus Christ, and make not provision for the flesh, to fulfill the lusts thereof.

Romans 13:14 (KJV)

We must put on Christ. How can we make it through life without putting on Christ? How can we make it to heaven without putting on Christ? Can one defeat sin without putting on Jesus? Can one receive a new life without putting on Jesus? Can one be a part of the body of Christ without putting on Christ? The answers should be easily and unanimously agreed on. The answers are all resoundingly "NO."

Jesus is the only one who can save you from sin. Jesus is the only one who can give you a new life. Jesus is the only door to heaven. You must turn to Him; you must submit to Him, and you must put on the name of Jesus Christ. How do we do this? Through baptism. We put on Jesus through baptism, when we are baptized by water in the name of Jesus, we are taking on the name of Jesus Christ.

For as many of you as have been baptized into Christ have put on Christ.

Galatians 3:27 (KJV)

You cannot be washed from your sins without putting on Jesus through baptism in His name. Don't reject the Gospel He gave His life for, rather submit to His plan and enter the joy of the Lord. Come to the cross and receive the blood, water, and Spirit of Jesus Christ that still flows from the savior.

Baptism in Jesus Name

There's a right way to be baptized. The efficacy of your baptism depends entirely on the name in which they baptized you. The power isn't in the water; the power is in the name.

Please read this and consider with earnest. You must be baptized in Jesus's name. No other name can save you, only the name of Jesus can. A grave misunderstanding of scripture has led modern Christianity to a false conclusion that baptism doesn't require the name of Jesus. Rather, baptism is to be administered in the name of the Father, Son, and Holy Spirit.

It's a misinterpretation of Matthew 28:19 that's led to this mass confusion. It's crucial you get this next part. For the sake of clarity, I will write plainly and clearly. I believe with all my heart that this world is heading toward a revelation of the truth in Jesus's name baptism.

We've already established baptism was important to Jesus and the first church of the book of Acts. More than just important; it was essential for God's plan of salvation; it was part of the proper response to the Gospel.

We need to go one step further though, because not only is baptism essential for salvation, you must be baptized correctly for salvation. Remember the boat God instructed Noah to build for the saving of his family with me. It wasn't enough for Noah to build a boat; Noah needed to build God's boat, God's way. Any other boat design wouldn't have worked for God's plan of salvation for Noah. Only God's design would be sufficient for their salvation.

It's the same with baptism, we must be baptized with His baptism. His way is the only way. Let's begin with the scripture that's created some confusion,

Go ye therefore, and teach all nations, baptizing them in the name of the Father, and of the Son, and of the Holy Ghost:

Matthew 28:19 (KJV)

Let me begin by saying this: we don't need to interpret this verse because this verse has already been interpreted for us. The people standing in front of Jesus as He spoke; the men and women who heard Him give those instructions, they interpreted His words for us. Here is why the apostles (the men who were sitting crisscross applesauce on the grass listening to Jesus talk) took Jesus's instructions, obeyed them, and carried out Jesus's words.

Every single baptism in the New Testament was done in the name of Jesus Christ. Peter baptized in Jesus's name, Ananias baptized in Jesus's name, Philip baptized in Jesus's name, and Paul baptized in Jesus's name.

Jesus led His disciples to the top of a hill and gives them His last instructions, His parting commission. Jesus spoke as the disciples listened intently and He told them to baptize in the name of the Father, and of the Son, and of the Holy Ghost, and when Jesus said those words, the disciples looked at one another and said "we must baptize in Jesus name"

It's abundantly clear that the apostles understood the command as baptize in Jesus's name, because not a single person in scripture was ever baptized in the name of the Father, Son, and Holy Ghost. Instead, here's what we read in scripture:

Then Peter said unto them, Repent, and <u>be baptized</u> every one of you <u>in the name of Jesus Christ</u> for the remission of sins, and ye shall receive the gift of the Holy Ghost.

Acts 2:38 (KJV)

> *For as yet he was fallen upon none of them: only <u>they were baptized in the name of the Lord Jesus.</u>*
>
> **Acts 8:16 (KJV)**

> *And he commanded them to be <u>baptized in the name of the Lord</u>. Then prayed they him to tarry certain days.*
>
> **Acts 10:48 (KJV)**

> *When they heard this, they were baptized in the name of the Lord Jesus.*
>
> **Acts 19:5 (KJV)**

> *And now why tarriest thou? arise, and be baptized, and wash away thy sins, <u>calling on the name of the Lord.</u>*
>
> **Acts 22:16 (KJV)**

This is how the apostles understood the command of Jesus Christ, so how can we interpret baptism in any other way? Do we know better than Peter and the apostles? We must let God be true and every man a liar.

Here's a common question: "does it really matter?" There's only one name with the power to save humanity. It's the name of Jesus Christ. There isn't another name sufficient for your salvation. When we pray for the sick, we pray in the name of Jesus Christ. Why? Because the power to heal the sick is in the name. When we baptize, we must baptize in Jesus's name because the power to wash away sins doesn't come from the water, it comes from the name of Jesus Christ.

Neither is there salvation in any other: <u>for there is none other name</u> under heaven given among men, whereby we must be saved.

Acts 4:12 (KJV)

Jesus is the only name given for our salvation. There isn't another saving option outside of Jesus. Jesus is the only door, and He's the only way. Be baptized the way they did it in the Bible, in Jesus's name.

Okay, well, how do you interpret Matthew 28:19? We must interpret it the same way His disciples interpreted it. When Jesus commanded baptism in the name of the Father and of the Son and of the Holy Ghost, they understood that to be in the name of Jesus Christ. Here is why, THERE IS A NAME.

Father, Son, and Spirit, they're not names; rather, they're relational titles. For example, I'm a father to my children; I'm a son to my parents; I'm a husband to my wife, and I'm a pastor to my congregation, but those aren't my name. My name isn't father, or son, or husband, my name is James. God is the Father of all creation. However, His name isn't "Father." So, when Jesus says baptize in the NAME of the Father, and of the Son, and of the Holy Ghost, the emphasis is on the singular name of the one who operates in all of those relational roles.

This isn't a book on the oneness of God, so I won't go too far into this. There's one name that covers all of whom God is, and that is Jesus. Jesus is the Son (Matt. 1:21), Jesus is the Father, (John 5:43, John 14), and Jesus is the Spirit (2 Corinthians 3:17). For more information on this, I recommend reading *The Oneness of God* by David K. Bernard.

Grammatically speaking, the command of Jesus was "baptize in the *name*." Everything that followed the name was a description of the name. Let me give an example I use when teaching. If I wrote you a check for one million dollars, and I made the check out to yourself, then I signed the check "Father," would it be valid? Of course not. What if I signed the check "Son?" Would it be valid? No, because even though I'm a father and a son, my name is James and without my name on the check, you can't cash it. It's my name that validates the check. The name validates your baptism. If you want salvation, you must have the name of Jesus written on your life. Jesus is the *only* name that can save.

This isn't a new thing. However, this is the only way the early church baptized for the first two hundred plus years of its existence. Until the Catholic Church changed the baptismal formula, and we recorded this in history. Of course, we don't look to history for our doctrines; we look to the scripture. We can look to history to help solidify the doctrines of scripture. Let me list a few statements about early baptism from encyclopedias.

The baptismal formula was changed from the name of JESUS CHRIST to the words Father, Son, & Holy Ghost by the Catholic Church in the second century.

Britannica Encyclopedia—11th Edition, Vol 3, Pg 365-366

Everywhere in the oldest sources it states that baptism took place in the name of Jesus Christ

Britannica Encyclopedia—Vol 3, Pg 82

The early church always baptized in the name of the Lord Jesus until development of Trinity doctrine in the 2nd century.

CANNEY ENCYCLOPEDIA OF RELIGION—Pg 53

Christian baptism was administered using the words "In the name of Jesus."

HASTINGS ENCYCLOPEDIA OF RELIGION—Vol 2, Pg 377

The use of a Trinitarian formula of any sort was not suggested in early Church history.

Vol 2, Pg 378

Baptism was always in the name of Lord Jesus until the time of Justin Martyr when Triune formula was used.

Vol 2, Pg 389

Biblically speaking, the church baptized in Jesus's name. Historically speaking, the church baptized in Jesus's name. God's plan is perfect, it doesn't need to be improved. Jesus always has been and always will be the only saving name. Make sure His name is on the check. I end this chapter with the direct words of the Apostle Peter "Repent and be baptized everyone of you in the name of Jesus Christ…"

10
The Gift

Greater is he that is in you, than he that is in the world.

—The Apostle John

What if I told you there's something greater than having God with you? One of the greatest revelations one can receive in life is a revelation of God's faithfulness. God is forever faithful and always constant. His faithfulness stands like the mountains; His compassion is as sure as the sunrise of a morning; His goodness is a guarantee; He's merciful, and He's gracious; He's truer than the laws of nature.

While gravity holds you down, His hands hold you up. Every night you lie your head down to sleep, it's the Lord who keeps every system in your body functioning. If there's breath in your lungs, it's because God put it there. If your heart is beating, it's because God set the rhythm. When you look around you, it's easy to see the evidence of God's faithfulness. In every season of life, God is with you.

People will change, seasons will change, circumstances will change, but God always remains the same.

God never changes. He's constant; Unwavering; Unmoving. He's always good; He's always faithful; He's the ultimate truth. He never leaves; He never forsakes. He's solid ground when all else is shaking; He's light when all else is in shadow. He's merciful; He's loving. Full of compassion, He cares for you and me. He is the Lord, strong and mighty, and He's right where you are.

You may not see Him, nor feel Him, but He is there. He surrounds you; He goes before you and behind you. He's to your left and to your right. His presence is with you always. There's never a moment where God is absent. Look back over your life. There's never been a minute God wasn't in it.

God is always with us. In the good, He's there. In the bad, He's there. It's one of the greatest revelations one can ever receive! The revelation is that God is always with us. But it's not the greatest revelation.

I'm so thankful God never leaves us, nor does He forsake us, but there's something so much greater than having God with you: it's having God *in* you. The Bible calls it "the gift of the Holy Ghost." God's greatest gift to us is the opportunity to make our lives His home.

Know ye not that ye are the temple of God, and that the Spirit of God dwelleth in you?

1 Corinthians 3:16 (KJV)

Christ in You

The greatest gift and the grandest opportunity in life is to be filled with the Spirit of the God of glory. There is nothing greater. There's nothing even close. It's comforting to know God is with you, but it's empowering to have God in you. This is what John said in his letter:

> *Ye are of God, little children, and have overcome them: because greater is he that is in you, than he that is in the world.*
>
> **1 John 4:4 (KJV)**

John wrote, "greater is he that is *in* you, than he that is in the world." John didn't say, "I'm bigger and stronger than any devil that may come against me." No, rather John declared there was someone inside him that was greater than anything in the world.

You cannot say what John said if you aren't filled with God's Spirit. If you don't have the gift of the Holy Ghost, then the statement is: "Greater is he that's in the world, then he that's me." Why? Because my human spirit isn't strong enough to resist temptation and sin. My human spirit is vulnerable to anxiety and depression. If I'm not full of God's Spirit, and all I have within me is my spirit, then I cannot stand against the enemies in the world. The enemy can stand against me; the devil can fight against me and my spirit, but if I'm full of God's Spirit, the devil cannot stand.

It's empowering to know there's no devil in or out of hell that can stand against the Lord. There's no drug addiction that God's Spirit cannot break. No fear too strong and no depression too great for the Holy Ghost.

We need God's Spirit on the inside. First, for salvation, which we'll talk about in a moment, but we also need the gift of the Holy Ghost to live victorious through the innumerable struggles we are facing and will face in our future.

Paul writes with such powerful words when he says:

To whom God would make known what is the riches of the glory of this mystery among the Gentiles; which is <u>Christ in you, the hope of glory</u>.

Colossians 1:27 (KJV)

The riches of glory are to have Christ in you! Not just with you, but in you. Paul said it's "the hope of glory." My hope is built on the amazing truth that my savior lives within me.

If we have the God's Spirit inside of us, we have power over the enemy. If we don't have the Spirit, we're powerless against the enemies and opposers that come against us. Jesus admonishes His disciples with this statement:

But ye shall receive power, after that the Holy Ghost is come upon you: and ye shall be witnesses unto me both in Jerusalem, and in all Judaea, and in Samaria, and unto the uttermost part of the earth.

Acts 1:8 (KJV)

You *will* receive power *after* the Holy Ghost. It isn't a chance that you'll receive power, but it's a guarantee. You'll receive power after the Holy Ghost. There's nothing else in life that can do for you what the Spirit will do.

You can have power over anxiety; you don't have to live in fear. You can have power over depression; you don't have to cope with the dark. You can have power over doubt; you don't have to live in confusion.

You don't have to follow a complicated formula or repeat a set of steps. You only need to open your heart and let God in. Let Him take away the spirit of fear and give you a spirit of power, love, and a sound mind (2 Timothy 1:7).

It's not enough to only have God with you; you need God in you. Yes, He is before me and behind me, and He's to my left and to my right. He surrounds me and walks with me, and I am *never* alone! But there's more: He's in my heart; He's in my mind; He's in my emotions; He knows my inner struggles, the many problems no one else knows about, the secret emotions and hidden thoughts. God knows them and is mighty enough to save me from those struggles. He can do the same for you. Let Him in.

The Big "if"

We know God is always with us, but the bigger question proves to be, is He in you? No matter where we are in life, we have God by our side. God promised Himself to us. He's promised us His faithfulness. We don't ever need to worry about whether we have God. Rather, we need to worry if He has us. He's given Himself to us, but have we given ourselves to Him?

There are things completely unavailable to us if we're not filled with the Spirit of God. We can find comfort in knowing God is with us, but we can have power in having God in us.

When you're filled with the gift of His Spirit, He can give you peace that passes understanding. He can give you a joy that's unspeakable and full of glory. He can empower you to be a better parent, a better spouse, and a better friend.

The biggest thing, however, is this: when you are filled with His Spirit, you receive new life. If you're living without the Holy Ghost, you're living dead in sin or powerless over the many evils around you, but when you open your heart and your mind and let the God of heaven and earth come into your life, you receive power to overcome evil. You receive a new life. It is contingent, however!

There's a big "if" in scripture.

> *But ye are not in the flesh, but in the Spirit, IF so be that the Spirit of God dwell in you. Now IF any man have not the Spirit of Christ, he is none of his. And IF Christ be in you, the body is dead because of sin; but the Spirit is life because of righteousness. But IF the Spirit of him that raised up Jesus from the dead dwell in you, he that raised up Christ from the dead shall also quicken your mortal bodies by his Spirit that dwelleth in you.*
>
> **Romans 8:9–11 (KJV)**

If the Spirit of God dwells in you, you will have life! The Spirit of Christ can raise you up, just like the beaten and bruised body of our messiah rose. We too can be resurrected to new life. God can take our depression and give us joy. He can take our pain and give us peace. He can take our messed up story full of tragedy and shameful mistakes, and He can rewrite the story. He can resurrect the hope missing in your heart. He can give a new life to your emotions. He can do whatever needs done *if* we let Him in.

There's no addiction you cannot overcome *if* you have the Holy Ghost. There's no family too broken that God cannot fix *if* we have the Holy Ghost. There's no mind God cannot calm *if* we have the Spirit of God living inside of us.

I want to say what John said, "greater is He that is in me than he that is in the world." But I cannot say that unless I have the Lord inside of me. I must be filled with the gift of the Holy Ghost.

Salvation

When Jesus ascended, He gave His disciples parting instructions. Jesus told His followers to go to Jerusalem and wait there for the "promise of the Father."

And, being assembled together with them, commanded them that they should not depart from Jerusalem, but wait for the promise of the Father, which, saith he, ye have heard of me. For John truly baptized with water; but ye shall be baptized with the Holy Ghost not many days hence.

Acts 1:4–5 (KJV)

The "promise of the Father" was the baptism of the Holy Ghost. Jesus, in His departure, gave them explicit instructions: "Go to Jerusalem and wait for the Spirit." The wording of the Scripture shows us that Jesus "Commanded them that they should not depart from Jerusalem." Don't leave Jerusalem until you receive the promise of the Father. Don't leave the city until you are baptized with the Holy Ghost.

Being filled with the Spirit of God isn't an option, it's a biblical command that came from the mouth of the Lord Jesus

Christ. In John chapter 3, Jesus said that one cannot enter the kingdom of heaven without being born of the Spirit.

Jesus answered, Verily, verily, I say unto thee, Except a man be born of water and of the Spirit, he cannot enter into the kingdom of God.

John 3:5 (KJV)

The most important reason we must be filled with God's Spirit is for the sake of salvation. If we're going to be saved, it must be God's way. His word must be the foundation for our salvation. His word tells me that without being born of the Spirit, I cannot enter the kingdom of heaven.

We must put God's word on a whole other level from man's word. God's word is so much higher and truer than anything man could ever say. So, when the Lord Jesus Christ says, "unless a man is born of water and of Spirit." We must take that word and hold it higher than all the lies surrounding us. It doesn't matter how eloquently a preacher can preach or teacher teach. God's word is always greater, and it's always true.

You can sit and listen to the most well-prepared lesson with beautiful wording and excellent presentation, but if the lesson's content disagrees with the teachings of Christ, we must regard it as false.

There's a way to salvation; it's through Jesus Christ. No other way to God besides Jesus Christ. No other words have eternal life, except for the words of our great God. And His word says we must be filled with His Spirit.

So, they waited. They tarried together in an upper room and, in a unified effort, they prayed for the promise of the Father. They didn't leave. No matter how uncomfortable it got, they stayed. No matter how bad the room stank, they remained, and they waited.

As days passed, you'd think their resolve would waver. They'd give up. They'd quit. They'd leave for the comforts of their homes, but they didn't. They stayed until God showed up.

They knew if God said He was coming, then He was coming. If God promised, He 'd come through. They waited, and they waited, and they waited. Then it happened.

And when the day of Pentecost was fully come, they were all with one accord in one place. And suddenly there came a sound from heaven as of a rushing mighty wind, and it filled all the house where they were sitting. And there appeared unto them cloven tongues like as of fire, and it sat upon each of them. And they were all filled with the Holy Ghost, and began to speak with other tongues, as the Spirit gave them utterance.

Acts 2:1-4 (KJV)

Then the day came. The day of Pentecost, the disciples were gathered in faith and obedience to God's command and God poured His Spirit on all who were in the room, and they were "filled with the Holy Ghost."

The promise always comes. If we put our trust in God, He'll always come through. He will answer your prayer. They waited as Jesus commanded for the promise of the Father. What they finally received was the infilling of the Holy Ghost, or the Spirit of God. The Holy Ghost is God's promise to His people. The promise is God with us and in us.

Notice this receiving God's Spirit depended on their obedience to His command. They were commanded to wait in Jerusalem until they received the promise. If they would've waited in any other town, they would've missed the outpouring of God's Spirit on the day of Pentecost. Only those men and women willing to hear God's word and obey God's word were filled with the Holy Ghost at that moment. Later in that same chapter, thousands more received God's salvation because they obeyed the command of the Apostle Peter. (See Acts 2:37–41.)

Salvation requires obedience. If we put our faith in God's word and obey what He commanded us to do, then we, too, can receive God's unparalleled promise, the gift of His Spirit living in us.

Biblical salvation includes receiving God's gift, the gift of His Spirit living in us.

Speaking in Tongues

The Bible teaches us that when you're filled with the Holy Spirit, there will be initial outward evidence of speaking in tongues. Perhaps one of the most common questions Pentecostals are asked are questions about speaking in tongues.

Also, an extremely common misconception about Pentecostals is that we believe you must speak in tongues to be saved. However, we do *not* believe that. We believe you must be filled with the Holy Ghost to be saved. That is clearly what the New Testament teaches. The New Testament also teaches that when you're filled with the Holy Ghost, speaking in tongues will accompany the experience.

And they were all filled with the Holy Ghost, and began to speak with other tongues, as the Spirit gave them utterance.
Acts 2:4 (KJV)

While Peter yet spake these words, the Holy Ghost fell on all them which heard the word. And they of the circumcision which believed were astonished, as many as came with Peter, because that on the Gentiles also was poured out the gift of the Holy Ghost. For they heard them speak with tongues, and magnify God. Then answered Peter,
Acts 10:44-46 (KJV)

And when Paul had laid his hands upon them, the Holy Ghost came on them; and they spake with tongues, and prophesied.
Acts 19:6 (KJV)

Speaking in tongues is evidence of God filling you with His Spirit. It's what happened all throughout the book of Acts with the apostles and the early church, and it's still the same today. We're not filled with a different Spirit; we're filled with the same Spirit, and we'll have the same experience.

Don't pursue speaking in tongues, pursue the gift of the Holy Ghost and when it happens, God's Spirit will bear witness with your spirit and you will speak in tongues as the Spirit gives the utterance.

What is it? It's God's Spirit speaking through you and out of you. It's outward evidence of an inward experience. Here's an analogy I like to give: I have terrible seasonal allergies. There are days the air quality suffers from pollen or ragweed that I sneeze uncontrollably. When I have an allergy attack, I must take medicine and lay down to try to alleviate the problem.

My sneezing is *not* the problem, the problem is that irritants have entered my nasal cavity and are triggering a bodily reaction. My sneezing is just evidence that something is happening inside of me. It's the same with the Holy Ghost. Speaking in tongues is outward evidence that something is happening inside of you.

Pursue the Holy Ghost. God wants to make your heart His home. You need the Spirit of God inside of you to make it heaven. Paul said regarding this, "We have this treasure in earthen vessels that the excellency of the power may be of God, and not of us." We can have the greatest treasure inside our clay vessel. May we never make the vessel the treasure. He is the treasure, not me.

11
Born to Live

The two most important days in your life are the days you are born and the day you find out why.

—Mark Twain

For this final chapter, I'd like to switch my focus. I want to issue a challenge to you. A challenge to not live below your potential in the Spirit. My desire for this conclusion is to encourage you to walk in the power and authority God has given us.

We have traveled through the stories of the Old and New Testaments of the Bible. I want to visit them once more; I want to pass by them to point out one more important theme we see written so carefully in the story. Forgive me if I don't spend ample time on these characters so deserving of it.

Let's go back to Abraham, Isaac, and Jacob: the three patriarchs of the Old Testament. Many times, when God is referenced, He's called "The God of Abraham, Isaac, and Jacob." These three men were the beginning of the nation of Israel. They're so central to the greater story that their names are used to describe the one true God. The God of Abraham, Isaac, and Jacob.

It's so powerful to me that God chose those three men as His identifiers. Out of all the prominent men and women of the Old Testament, He chose to be known by those three men. He is the God of Abraham, Isaac, and Jacob.

It's so powerful because each of those three men experienced supernatural births. Abraham married Sarah. She was barren, but God gave her a miracle and she conceived at ninety. Isaac married Rebekah, and she was also barren, but God healed her body and gave them twin boys. Jacob married Rachel and once again, she too was unable to bear children until God gave her a miracle and she gave birth.

Each of those three men experienced a supernatural birth. Each of them gave birth to the next generation through a miraculous working of God's power. The principle is this: the God of Abraham, Isaac, and Jacob is the God of the supernatural birth. Every time God is called by the names of the three patriarchs, He's being identified as the God of the supernatural birth.

This thread doesn't end with Jacob. We see it in multiple places within the Old Testament. Hannah is barren, but she prays until God answers and heals her body. She miraculously gives birth to Samuel, who would later be the prophet who anointed David to be the king. Jesus is referred to as "the son of David," and Jerusalem is "the city of David." The man who wrote the largest portion of our Bible, he was anointed by a prophet who was born supernaturally.

Of course, we must mention John the Baptist, who was the messenger who came and prepared the earth for the coming messiah. He, too, was born supernaturally from a barren woman of old age.

Then it all culminates in the world's savior, Jesus Christ. His was the most supernatural of them all because there was nothing natural about His conception. A young virgin would conceive by the Holy Ghost and bear a child. His mother would be Mary, but His father was the Lord God of Israel. He'd then preach to others that they must be born again of the Spirit.

He is the Lord of the supernatural birth. He has made a way for us to be born supernaturally through His Spirit. If you are filled with His Spirit, then you receive new life; you've been born again in the most supernatural way possible. You are His child.

Living in Power

Here is the challenge and the entire point of this closing chapter; we weren't born supernaturally just to live naturally. We weren't born of the Spirit just so we can continue to live in the flesh. But we were born supernaturally, so we may live supernaturally. He has given us His power and His authority. We must commit ourselves to living in that power and authority.

Never be comfortable living underneath the level of the supernatural. God can work miracles through you. You have the power of Jesus inside of you. Pray for your family, pray for your friends. America needs men and women living in the power of the Holy Spirit. We need to pray for our cities and our country. There's only one thing that can save America: it is Jesus Christ, and you have Him.

Now unto him that is able to do exceeding abundantly above all that we ask or think, according to the power that worketh in us.

Ephesians 3:20 (KJV)

God can do anything that needs to be done. He's greater than any struggle, stronger than any disease. His grace is sufficient for the sins of the entire world. The world will never be too wicked or too dark for God to make a difference. He is able; He is able; He is able, but it is all according to the power that works in us.

The power to heal our nation is locked inside of born again Christians. The power to save the lost on every continent is locked inside of born again believers. We must exercise the power in us. Pray in the Spirit, walk in the Spirit, go to work in the Spirit, go to school in the Spirit, and go in the Spirit to your lost family and to your lost city. Watch what God will do through you.

You are born supernaturally to live supernaturally. Increase your faith in the wonderworking God. Step out in boldness and declare healing for yourself and others. Prophesy and pray for revival, and watch as Pentecost sweeps through your city and your church.

I am so honored that you gave me your time. I pray you are blessed by what you have read. I pray God's blessings on you and on your family. Remember, let God be true and every man a liar.

And I say also unto thee, That thou art Peter, and upon this rock I will build my church; and the gates of hell shall not prevail against it. And I will give unto thee the keys of the kingdom of heaven: and whatsoever thou shalt bind on earth shall be bound in heaven: and whatsoever thou shalt loose on earth shall be loosed in heaven.

Matthew 16:18-19 (KJV)

Made in the USA
Columbia, SC
18 June 2024